THE ESSENTIAL BOOK OF

USELESS
INFORMATION

THE ESSENTIAL BOOK OF
USELESS
INFORMATION

THE MOST UNIMPORTANT THINGS YOU'LL NEVER NEED TO KNOW

DON VOORHEES

A PERIGEE BOOK

A PERIGEE BOOK
Published by the Penguin Group
Penguin Group (USA) Inc.
375 Hudson Street, New York, New York 10014, USA
Penguin Group (Canada), 90 Eglinton Avenue East, Suite 700, Toronto, Ontario M4P 2Y3, Canada
(a division of Pearson Penguin Canada Inc.)
Penguin Books Ltd., 80 Strand, London WC2R 0RL, England
Penguin Group Ireland, 25 St. Stephen's Green, Dublin 2, Ireland (a division of Penguin Books Ltd.)
Penguin Group (Australia), 250 Camberwell Road, Camberwell, Victoria 3124, Australia
(a division of Pearson Australia Group Pty. Ltd.)
Penguin Books India Pvt. Ltd., 11 Community Centre, Panchsheel Park, New Delhi—110 017, India
Penguin Group (NZ), 67 Apollo Drive, Rosedale, North Shore 0632, New Zealand
(a division of Pearson New Zealand Ltd.)
Penguin Books (South Africa) (Pty.) Ltd., 24 Sturdee Avenue, Rosebank, Johannesburg 2196,
South Africa

Penguin Books Ltd., Registered Offices: 80 Strand, London WC2R 0RL, England

While the author has made every effort to provide accurate telephone numbers and Internet addresses at the time of publication, neither the publisher nor the author assumes any responsibility for errors, or for changes that occur after publication. Further, the publisher does not have any control over and does not assume any responsibility for author or third-party websites or their content.

PRINTING HISTORY
Perigee trade paperback edition / November 2009
Perigee trade paperback holiday edition / October 2010

Perigee trade paperback holiday edition ISBN: 978-0-399-53652-6

The Library of Congress has cataloged the Perigee trade paperback edition as follows:

Voorhees, Don.
   The essential book of useless information : the most unimportant things you'll never need to know / Don Voorhees.—1st ed.
      p.   cm.
   ISBN 978-0-399-53536-9 (trade pbk.)
   1. Curiosities and wonders. I. Title.
   AG243.V66 2009
   031.02—dc22   2009025315

PRINTED IN THE UNITED STATES OF AMERICA

10 9 8 7 6 5 4 3 2 1

Most Perigee books are available at special quantity discounts for bulk purchases for sales promotions, premiums, fund-raising, or educational use. Special books, or book excerpts, can also be created to fit specific needs. For details, write: Special Markets, Penguin Group (USA) Inc., 375 Hudson Street, New York, New York 10014.

To my beautiful wife, Lisa, for living with a know-it-all these many years.

CONTENTS

MASCOT MUSINGS

The word "squirrel" comes from the Greek *skiouros*, meaning "shadow-tailed," because they use their tails to keep warm or shade themselves from the sun.

Some squirrels are predatory.

A squirrel's teeth grow continuously and they gnaw to wear them down.

Squirrels are believed to have twice knocked out the NASDAQ market. In 1987, a squirrel caused a transformer power surge, shutting the exchange down for eighty-two minutes. In 1994, another squirrel chewed through a power line, disrupting trading for thirty-two minutes.

Presidential candidate Mike Huckabee used to fry squirrels in a popcorn maker he had in his college dorm.

Squirrel meat is high in cholesterol.

Some people in the backwoods of Kentucky consider squirrel brains a delicacy.

The eastern gray squirrel is legally classified as vermin in Britain.

THE BOOB TUBE

BEFORE HI-DEF

A Russian scientist—Constantin Perskyi—first coined the word "television" at the 1900 Paris World's Fair, when referring to the transmission of still photographs through electrical wires.

General Electric introduced the first American TV set in 1928.

The first remote control—called Lazy Bones—was sold by Zenith in 1950. It was connected to the set by a wire.

Color TVs became available in 1951, but most people didn't have one until the 1960s.

The first show nationally televised in color was the 1954 New Year's Day Tournament of Roses Parade on NBC.

By 1966, all new network programs were broadcast in color.

In 1967, the U.S. Congress mandated PBS (Public Broadcasting Service). It began broadcasting in 1970.

The Corporation for Public Broadcasting receives 15 to 20 percent of its annual operating revenue from federal sources and 25 to 29 percent from state and local taxes.

Home Box Office (HBO), the first pay cable network, went on the air in 1972.

In 1974, two-thirds of American homes had color TVs.

In 1986, FOX became America's fourth broadcast network. In the 2007–2008 season, FOX became the nation's highest-rated network.

Television dials didn't have a channel 1 in the old days, because that frequency got too much interference. In 1948, the government reassigned the wavelength for taxicab company usage. It is now designated for amateur radio and mobile usage. Modern cable systems may have a channel 1, but they are not related to the original VHF channel 1 television frequency, except in name.

According to a *TV Guide* report, the best viewing distance from the TV depends on the size of the screen. The industry claims that for the sharpest picture people should sit at a distance of between four and eight times the height of the TV screen.

TV LAND

Almost three hundred TV comedy and drama series have exceeded the one-hundred-episode mark. Eighty-three have gone past two hundred episodes, while only twenty have surpassed three hundred episodes. Seven have eclipsed four hundred episodes, four topped five hundred episodes, and only *Gunsmoke* made it above six hundred.

Portly Pat Corley—Phil the Bartender on *Murphy Brown*—was once a ballet dancer. Many years and many pounds ago, he spent four seasons dancing with the Stockton Symphony Ballet in California.

Actor Caroll Spinney has been playing Big Bird since 1969.

Dick York played Darren for five seasons on *Bewitched*, until he had to retire from acting because of a back injury he had suffered earlier in his career, filming the western *They Came to Cordura*. Dick Sargent replaced him for the show's last three seasons.

None of the cast of *The Dick Van Dyke Show* was in the original pilot, not even Dick Van Dyke himself. The show's creator—Carl Reiner—played the lead. Johnny Carson almost ended up with the lead before Dick Van Dyke was picked.

Jim Carrey starred in the 1983 sitcom *The Duck Factory*, where he played a cartoonist.

George Carlin was the first guest host of *Saturday Night Live*, in 1975. Janis Ian was the first musical guest.

Jim Backus, who played Thurston Howell III on *Gilligan's Island*, was also the voice of Mr. Magoo.

"YOU GOT SOME 'SPLAININ' TO DO!"

I Love Lucy was a takeoff on a radio show that Lucille Ball was doing, called *My Favorite Husband*.

Lucille Ball has been on more *TV Guide* covers than anyone, and the magazine reports that her face has been seen by more people than anyone else's in history.

Lucy was a registered communist due to her socialist grandfather.

Lucy wanted her friend Barbara Peppers to play Ethel Mertz, but she was a chronic alcoholic and was passed over for Vivian Vance. Lucy had reservations about casting Vance because she was younger than Lucy, very beautiful, and was supposed to play frumpy Ethel. Vance wore makeup and put on weight to make her appear dowdy.

William Frawley and Vivian Vance, who played the Mertzes, despised each other. She hated him so much that she turned down a Mertz spin-off show, despite a large salary offer.

William Frawley was a notorious drinker and was contractually bound to complete sobriety during the show's production.

William Frawley was such a big Yankees fan that he stipulated in his contract that if they made the World Series he could fly back to New York to attend the games. This happened seven times during the show's nine seasons.

Desi Arnaz instituted the idea of reruns, when he had the network re-air early episodes of the show after Lucy gave birth.

"ONE OF THESE DAYS, ALICE!"

The only cast member of *The Honeymooners* to receive residuals from the show was Audrey Meadows. She received royalty checks on reruns of *The Honeymooners* from 1955 until her death in 1996.

Audrey Meadows replaced Pert Kelton, the original actress who played Alice when *The Honeymooners* was just a skit on *The Jackie Gleason Show*. Kelton had been blacklisted.

Alice's maiden name was Gibson.

The shows were never fully rehearsed since Jackie Gleason liked spontaneity.

Jackie Gleason would pat his stomach whenever he forgot a line.

"I SEE NOTHING!"

Many of the actors on *Hogan's Heroes* were Jews who'd fled the Nazis during World War II—Werner Klemperer (Klink), John Banner (Schultz), Robert Clary (LeBeau), Leon Askin (General Burkhalter), and Howard Caine (Major Hochstetter). Robert Clary was held three years in a concentration camp and had an identity tattoo from the camp on his arm. John Banner and Clary both had parents and family members exterminated in the war.

Bob Crane, who played Colonel Hogan, also played drums on the song at the show's opening. It is called "Hogan's Heroes March" and has lyrics.

Several of the cast members released an album titled *Hogan's Heroes Sing the Best of World War II*.

"SHUT UP, DUMMY!"

Redd Foxx's given name was John Elroy Sanford. His brother's name was Fred Sanford, which he used for the sitcom *Sanford and Son*. He was called Redd because of his reddish hair and complexion.

Redd Foxx's mother was half-Seminole.

Redd Foxx began his comedy career introducing strippers in the 1950s.

Redd Foxx was a close friend of Malcolm X.

When Redd Foxx died of a heart attack during a rehearsal break on the TV show *The Royal Family*, the cast members thought he was doing the "I'm coming, Elizabeth!" fake heart attack shtick that he was famous for.

"BEAM ME UP, SCOTTY"

Captain Kirk never said, "Beam me up, Scotty," in any episode of *Star Trek*.

Lloyd Bridges and Jack Lord both turned down an offer to play the part of Kirk.

Aluminum powder blown by a fan provided the shimmer of the transporter beam.

Star Trek never made it higher than number fifty-two in the ratings.

The *Star Trek* theme song has lyrics.

William Shatner recorded a spoken-word album in 1969—*The Transformed Man*—on which he delivered interpretive recitations of "Lucy in the Sky with Diamonds" and "Mr. Tambourine Man," backed by an orchestra.

Star Trek creator Gene Roddenberry and his wife will have their ashes launched into deep space in 2010.

MARSHA, JEANNIE, AND BRIDGET

The kids' bathroom on *The Brady Bunch* had no toilet.

For the first couple of seasons, Barbara Eden had to hide her navel on *I Dream of Jeannie*, for fear of being censored. It does briefly slip out a few times on some episodes.

The highest rated TV show ever to be canceled was *Bridget Loves Bernie* in 1973. CBS decided the country wasn't ready for this number-five-ranked sitcom about a mixed-religious marriage, after all the hate mail they got. Costars Meredith Baxter and David Birney were later married, after meeting on the set, in 1974. They divorced in 1989.

DINGBAT AND MEATHEAD

All in the Family was the first comedy series shot on tape instead of film.

All in the Family was rated number one for five consecutive years, a record only matched by *The Cosby Show*.

Mickey Rooney turned down perhaps the greatest comedic television role of the decade, when he passed on playing Archie on *All in the Family*.

Carroll O'Connor auditioned for the role of the Skipper on *Gilligan's Island*, which eventually went to Alan Hale Jr.

Harrison Ford turned down the role of Michael Stivic because he found Archie's bigotry to be too crude.

Rob Reiner, who played Michael, was balding so fast that he started wearing a toupee halfway through the first season.

Archie's chair was purchased for eight dollars at a Goodwill store. After *All in the Family*'s eighth season, show creator Norman Lear donated Archie and Edith's chairs for display in the Smithsonian. When the show was renewed for a ninth season, Lear had to have facsimiles created at a cost of several thousand dollars.

Carroll O'Connor and Jean Stapleton sing the show's opening theme seated at a piano because the producers couldn't afford an orchestra.

The first toilet flush heard on TV came from Archie's upstairs bathroom.

"WILBUUUR"

Mr. Ed's real name was Bamboo Harvester. He was a gelding (castrated male horse).

Bamboo's stable mate—a horse named Pumpkin—was Ed's stunt double on the show, and later a star in his own right, appearing on *Green Acres*.

Ed wouldn't respond to any of his costars, only to his trainer—Les Hilton—who would always be on the set to give him his cues.

When Ed was tired of working, he would just walk off the set.

GOOD, GIRL?

All of the *Lassie* dogs were male. The original collie cast by MGM to be Lassie was a female. The dog, however, refused to jump into a raging river in a certain scene. The studio then brought in a larger, stronger male dog named Pal, which had no problem with the demanding stunts. Male dogs were also used to portray Lassie because they retain a thicker summer coat, which looks better on TV.

There were seven *Lassie* movies before *Lassie* began airing on CBS for seventeen seasons.

Contrary to popular myth, Lassie never saved Timmy from falling down a well.

"NO SOUP FOR YOU!"

Seinfeld debuted as *The Seinfeld Chronicles* and was not expected to do well. NBC actually offered the show to FOX, which passed on it.

Kramer originally wore clothes from the 1960s to give the impression that he couldn't afford new ones, not to make him look retro. This is why his pants were always about an inch too short.

George's clothes were intentionally tailored one size too small to make him look geeky.

Danny DeVito was considered for the role of George.

Jonathan Wolff, who composed the music for *Seinfeld*, performed the popping noises heard during the credits and at commercial breaks.

The real life Soup Nazi of *Seinfeld* fame—Al Yeganeh—was so mad at Jerry Seinfeld that he refused to accept Jerry's heartfelt apology when he went to the International Soup Kitchen to make amends.

Lloyd Braun (a recurring character on *Seinfeld*) was the name of a real life ABC Entertainment executive.

In the first conversation of the first episode of *Seinfeld*, Jerry and George discuss a button. They also are talking about a button in the last conversation of the last episode.

"SUICIDE IS PAINLESS"

The *M*A*S*H* theme song is called "Suicide Is Painless." The lyrics were written by Mike Altman, the fourteen-year-old son of Robert Altman, the movie's director.

Gary Burghoff, who played Radar on *M*A*S*H*, was the only cast member to reprise his role from the hit movie.

Tim Brown, who played Corporal Judson in the movie, played Spearchucker Jones on the show.

Alan Alda (Hawkeye) and Jamie Farr (Klinger) both served in Korea after the war. Farr wore his actual dog tags on the show.

Hawkeye's name on *M*A*S*H* comes from the character in the book *The Last of the Mochicans*.

Actor Gary Burghoff has a deformed hand, so his character Radar O'Reilly's left hand was always either in his pocket or behind something. Occasionally a glimpse of his misshapen fingers could be seen.

The show's outdoor set, near Malibu, California, was destroyed by a brush fire at the end of the 1982 production season, so the show writers wrote the fire into the script.

McLean Stevenson (Henry) and Wayne Rogers (Trapper) both left the show because it focused too much on Alda's character for their taste.

"AAAY!"

The pilot for *Happy Days* was turned down by ABC but used in the anthology series *Love, American Style*. George Lucas liked Ron Howard's portrayal of Richie Cunningham and cast him in the blockbuster movie *American Graffiti*. After the success of the movie, ABC bought the show.

Anson Williams, who played teenager Potsie on *Happy Days*, was twenty-five in 1974, his first year on the show. When the show went off the air nine years later, the youthful Potsie was still played by the thirty-four-year-old actor.

"Jumping the shark" refers to the moment when a TV show has run out of new ideas and resorts to absurd story-lines. The expression comes from a crazy 1977 episode of *Happy Days*, where Fonzi dons swim trunks with his leather jacket and does a water ski jump over a penned-in shark.

During the first season and a half of *Happy Days*, Richie had an older brother Chuck. He was dropped from the show with no explanation. "Chuck Cunningham Syndrome" is now the expression for a character that mysteriously disappears from a TV show.

"D'OH!"

The characters on *The Simpsons* are named for members of creator Matt Groening's family. His parents are Homer and Marge, his sisters' names are Lisa and Maggie. The name Bart, appropriately enough, is an anagram for "brat."

The actors who do the voices on *The Simpsons* are paid $400,000 per episode.

DAILY DOUBLE

The second and third place finishers on *Jeopardy!* don't get the dollar value of their score. The second place contestant gets fifteen hundred dollars and one thousand dollars is awarded for third place. This helps offset their travel expenses to L.A., which the show does not pay.

The $75,000 won by Ken Jennings on July 23, 2004, is the biggest single day winnings yet on *Jeopardy!*

If no player finishes Final Jeopardy with at least one dollar, all three contestants lose. This has happened three times in modern *Jeopardy!*

There has been one three-way tie for first on *Jeopardy!*

Only one player ever won Final Jeopardy with just one dollar.

BUY A VOWEL

The first host of *Wheel of Fortune*, in 1975, was Chuck Woolery, with Susan Stafford turning the letters.

Pat Sajak was a local TV weatherman before he was discovered by Merv Griffin and selected to host *Wheel of Fortune*.

Vanna White has had numerous top designers supplying her with the 5,100 different outfits she's worn on the show so far. And no, they don't go home with her, they are auctioned off for charity.

QUIZ MASTERS

Bill Cullen and Winston "Wink" Martindale have both hosted sixteen game shows. Dick Clark and Alex Trebek have each hosted a dozen or so.

> Kirstie Alley won five thousand dollars as a contestant on *Match Game* and ten thousand dollars on *Password Plus*.

Robert Redford received a fishing pole as payment for appearing as a demonstrator on the show *Play Your Hunch* in 1959.

> According to Howie Mandel, the models on *Deal or No Deal* often faint as a result of standing so long under the hot lights.

"THIS JUST IN . . ."

Dan Rather once stormed off the set of his newscast, leaving six minutes of dead air, when he learned a tennis match would run a few minutes into the broadcast.

> Peter Jennings was a high school dropout.

Walter Cronkite, the dean of television anchormen, hosted the CBS game show *It's News to Me* in 1954.

VIDEO KILLED THE RADIO STAR

MTV actually played music videos at one time.

MTV debuted at midnight on August 1, 1981. It was no accident that they kicked off their network with the song "Video Killed the Radio Star" by the Buggles.

In 1992, MTV's *Real World* became the first American "reality" show.

BAD MUSIC

Jeff Conaway, of *Taxi* and *Grease* fame, recorded an album in 1980 called *Jeff Conaway*.

Another wacky album concept was 1964's *At Home with the Munsters*, featuring the cast singing.

Not to be outdone, in 1968 *The Beverly Hillbillies* album hit the stores.

"You're My Girl: Romantic Reflections by Jack Webb" was a real toe tapper. The deadpan *Dragnet* star read the "song" lyrics while an orchestra played in the background.

SOAP SUDS

The Guiding Light began as a radio program in 1937 and was on TV since 1952, before finally being canceled in 2009.

Robert De Niro, Dustin Hoffman, and Susan Sarandon all started their careers on the soap opera *Search for Tomorrow*. Bette Midler started on *The Edge of Night* and Kathleen Turner was on *The Doctors*. Sigourney Weaver acted on *Somerset*.

During the 1982–83 television season, Janine Turner and Demi Moore played the Templeton sisters on *General Hospital*. They both looked somewhat different than they do today. Turner had long blond hair and Moore was flat-chested!

Mia Farrow got her start on *Peyton Place*.

Jack Nicholson could be seen on different episodes of the late 1950s show *Divorce Court*. Jack usually played a reporter or the "other man."

CULTURE SHOCK

The Deadliest Catch was the favorite TV show of the prisoners in Guantánamo Bay.

Gitmo prisoners destroyed numerous TV sets that showed commercials of fully clothed women simply washing their arms.

WE'LL BE RIGHT BACK

Bulova Watch aired the first TV commercial, a ten-second "Bulova Watch Time" announcement on WBNT-NY (today's WNBC) on July 1, 1941. The spot cost all of nine dollars and was available to the about four thousand television sets in the New York area at that time.

Pepsi's "Like a Prayer" ad featuring Madonna, shot in 1992, cost $5 million to produce and was aired just once in the United States, as Pepsi found it to be too racy for their taste.

Miami Vice star Don Johnson was dumped as Pepsi's TV pitchman when he was photographed by *People* magazine drinking a Diet Coke. Oops!

James Dean did a Pepsi commercial.

The Macintosh computer was introduced to the world in a TV commercial that ran just once, during halftime of the Super Bowl in 1984. It is considered to be the greatest commercial of all time by *Advertising Age*.

Kate Winslet's first role was dancing with the Honey Monster in a Sugar Puffs cereal commercial.

Porn star Marilyn Chambers once appeared on the Ivory Soap box as the fresh-faced, young mother holding the cute baby.

During *The Flintstones'* first season, Fred, Barney, and Wilma smoked cigarettes in a Winston commercial that ran during the show.

Mr. Magoo drank Stag beer in commercials. (Now you know the real reason he was so clueless all the time.)

🌰 YEN FOR MONEY

Lots of the most "respected" American stars, who are "above" lowering themselves to hawking products for profit on domestic television commercials, have no problem doing so in Japan. Apparently, some are so embarrassed about it that they have secrecy clauses put in their contracts. The following is an abbreviated list of stars appearing in Japanese commercials:

Michael Jackson—Suzuki Scooters

Mike Tyson—beer

Harrison Ford—beer

Mariah Carey—coffee

Audrey Hepburn—cosmetics and tea

Arnold Schwarzenegger—energy drinks

Nicholas Cage—pachinko machines

Brad Pitt—Internet bank machines

George Clooney—Toyota

Sylvester Stallone—ham

YAK, YAK, YAK

The first early morning talk show was Philadelphia-based *Three to Get Ready*, hosted by Ernie Kovacs in 1949. It ran live, with no scripts or sets, and a prop budget of only fifteen dollars a week.

The Today Show has been on since 1952.

TALK SOUP

The waiting rooms for guests on TV shows are called "green rooms" because the waiting rooms for early theatrical performers just offstage *were* actually painted green. It was believed the color green would soothe the actors' eyes, which were strained by the bright theater lights. The rooms are rarely green now, but the name remains.

In 1971, seventy-two-year-old Rodale Press founder Jerome Rodale died while taping an interview on *The Dick Cavett Show*. Earlier in the interview, he'd announced that he never felt better in his life and would live to be a hundred.

Oprah makes all her employees sign lifelong confidentiality agreements.

Oprah is the third woman to own a TV production company—Mary Pickford and Lucille Ball did also.

Cohost of *Entertainment Tonight* Mary Hart has her legs insured for $1 million.

As reported in the *New England Journal of Medicine*, there is a woman who goes into epileptic seizures at the sound of Mary Hart's voice. This case was portrayed with much hilarity by the character Kramer on an episode of *Seinfeld*.

"HERE'S JOHNNY!"

The Tonight Show has been on since 1954.

Jackie Gleason, Bob Newhart, Groucho Marx, and Joey Bishop all turned down the job of replacing Jack Paar hosting *The Tonight Show*, before NBC asked Johnny Carson.

Groucho Marx was Johnny's first guest on *The Tonight Show*, in 1962.

When Johnny once joked in his monologue about a shortage of toilet paper, he caused a nationwide run on TP, creating an actual shortage.

FROM THE HOME OFFICE

David Letterman started out as an Indianapolis TV weatherman.

The Ed Sullivan Theatre, where *The Late Show with David Letterman* is taped, is kept at 58°F because Dave likes it that way.

Monday through Thursday shows are taped at 5:30 p.m. the day of the show. Friday shows are taped at 8:30 p.m. the day before.

Dave used to announce before reading his Top Ten List that it came "from the home office of Sioux City, Iowa," as a poke at the only CBS affiliate not to air the show.

Movie Madness

EXTRA CREDITS

The most tickets to the movies in America were sold in 1946—4 billion. About a third that number are bought today.

India produces more than one thousand movies a year, much more than the United States.

The first screen kiss was between May Irwin and John C. Rice, in the forty-seven-second-long 1896 film short *The Kiss*, produced by Thomas Edison.

The Blair Witch Project, which cost only $22,000 to make, grossed $248 million, making it the film with the highest box office sales to production cost ratio of all time.

Buster Crabbe played Buck Rogers, Flash Gordon, and Tarzan in the movies.

GIVEN NAMES

Did you know the full given names of these stars?

Mel Columcille Gerard Gibson

Jennifer Joanna Anastassakis (Aniston)

Ashley Tyler Ciminella (Judd)

Kiefer William Frederick Dempsey George Rufus Sutherland

Russell Ira Crowe

Orlando Jonathan Blanchard Bloom

Beyonce Giselle Knowles

Samuel Leroy Jackson

EXTRA BUTTER, PLEASE

Popcorn and Twizzlers are the favorite American movie snack foods.

Big surprise—95 percent of the price of a tub of popcorn at the movies is profit.

During the 1920s, popcorn was banned from the movies because it was too noisy.

More popcorn is sold during the showing of scary movies.

In parts of the South, they sell pickles at the movies.

Folks in Colombia eat fried ant bellies at the movies.

ON THE GOOD SHIP LOLLIPOP

Shirley Temple's mother did her hairpins every day, making sure that she always had exactly fifty-six curls.

Shirley was considered for the role of Dorothy in *The Wizard of Oz*.

She was so wildly popular that she received an estimated 167,000 presents on her ninth birthday.

Shirley is the only female star to have a drink named after her.

She stopped believing in Santa Claus at age six, when her mother took her to a department store to see St. Nick and he asked her for her autograph.

Shirley was number one at the box office for four years.

THE HILLS ARE ALIVE

During the filming of the opening scene of *The Sound of Music*, with Julie Andrews on top of the mountain, she kept getting thrown to the ground by the helicopter's downdraft.

Debbie Turner, who played Marta, had several loose

teeth during the filming, which kept falling out and had to be replaced with fakes.

Several future stars auditioned to play the von Trapp children, including Richard Dreyfuss (who couldn't dance), Kurt Russell, Patty Duke, Mia Farrow, Sharon Tate, Lesley Ann Warren, and four of the Osmond brothers.

Doris Day and Audrey Hepburn were considered for the role of Maria.

Yul Brenner, Sean Connery, and Richard Burton were considered for the role of Captain von Trapp.

Christopher Plummer, who played the Captain, intensely disliked working on the film and likened acting with Julie Andrews to "being hit over the head with a big Valentine's Day card."

The von Trapp house used in the movie actually belonged to Hedy Lamarr.

The movie is practically unknown in Austria, but there are tours of the film's locales for tourists.

To offer more showings, a South Korean movie theater once cut out all the songs to shorten the movie.

WE'RE NOT IN KANSAS ANYMORE

There have been thirty-nine book sequels to *The Wizard of Oz*, thirteen of them by L. Frank Baum.

The song "Over the Rainbow" was almost edited out of the movie.

Buddy Ebsen, of *The Beverly Hillbillies* fame, was originally cast as the Tin Man, but became critically ill nine days into the shoot from breathing in the aluminum powder that was used as makeup for the role.

Frank Morgan, who played the Wizard, also played Professor Marvel, the Emerald City gatekeeper, the Wizard's guard, and the cabbie of the Horse of a Different Color carriage.

The movie went through five directors before it was finished.

Margaret Hamilton, who played the Wicked Witch of the West, was a kindergarten teacher who adored children. She was severely burned during the special effect where she exits Munchkinland. A trapdoor, obscured by smoke, was supposed to drop her below the stage just before an eruption of flames shot up. On the first take, the trapdoor could be seen, so they set off the flames a little earlier for the second take, setting her costume on fire. The first take, with the trapdoor visible, is the one used in the movie.

TOO FAST TO LIVE . . .

Blue jeans became the rage with teens after James Dean wore them in the 1955 film *Rebel Without a Cause*.

James Dean was an avid racer. His Porsche 550 Spyder was nicknamed "Little Bastard." When Alec Guinness saw the car, he told Dean, "If you get in that car, you will be found dead in it by this time next week." Dean died in a wreck seven days later.

Shortly before Dean's fatal 1955 car accident near Cholame, California, he was pulled over for speeding. It is not believed he was speeding at the time of the crash.

Dean's passenger in the car—his mechanic Rolf Wütherich—was thrown from the wreck and survived, only to die in another accident in 1981.

Paul Newman got the next two movie roles that were slated for Dean after his death. He *was* going to give up acting and start directing.

Dean's estate still earns about $5 million a year.

OOPS!

Several of the major battle scenes in the movie *Braveheart* had to be re-shot when it was realized some of the extras were wearing wristwatches and sunglasses.

Stanley Kubrick made Shelley Duvall do 127 retakes of the baseball bat scene in *The Shining*.

In *Indiana Jones and the Kingdom of the Crystal Skull*, which is set in 1957, Indy fires an RPG-7 launcher that wasn't invented until 1961.

Space is a vacuum, so you shouldn't be able to see laser beams moving through it. They are only visible in a medium, like fog. Sorry, George Lucas.

Likewise, sound doesn't travel in space either, so you wouldn't hear engine noises or explosions. *2001: A Space Odyssey* is one of the few movies that accurately depicted the silence of space, to great effect.

Bullets generally don't spark when they hit metal, since they are made of a copper-clad lead.

BEHIND THE SCENES

The makeup budget for the movie *Planet of the Apes* was 17 percent of the total production costs.

A man's scream recorded for the 1951 movie *Distant Drums* has been used by sound libraries in more than seventy other films, including *Spider-Man*, *Toy Story*, and *The Lord of the Rings: The Two Towers*.

Most soundstages prohibit tobacco, so the actors usually smoke herbal cigarettes.

For years, movies used "glass" made out of sugar for actors to jump through. Now special plastic is used.

In the 1931 film *Little Caesar*, Edward G. Robinson could not keep his eyes open while firing a gun. They solved the problem by taping them open.

Renée Zellweger had to go from a size 6 to a size

14 for the lead role in *Bridget Jones's Diary* and its sequel.

American soprano Marni Nixon was the singing voice for Deborah Kerr in *The King and I*, Natalie Wood in *West Side Story*, and Audrey Hepburn in *My Fair Lady*.

WHO ARE THESE GUYS?

In the movie business, a gaffer is the head electrician. The key grip is the head lighting and rigging person on the set, so called because a strong grip is useful. The best boy is an assistant to the gaffer and key grip.

DYING TO GET SOME REST

Sarah Bernhardt, one of the most famous actresses of the late-nineteenth and early-twentieth centuries, slept in a coffin that she took with her wherever she went.

Jayne Mansfield was killed in 1967 when the car she was riding in rear-ended a tractor-trailer and under-rode it. Her daughter Mariska Hargitay and two siblings were in the backseat and survived with minor injuries. This accident prompted the installation of the under-ride bars on the back of all trucks today, known as "Mansfield bars."

OH, HENRY!

Henry Kissinger dated Candice Bergen, Jill St. John, Marlo Thomas, and Shirley MacLaine.

HELLO? THEY'RE CARTOONS!

In the old Disney cartoons, Minnie Mouse's friend Clarabelle Cow had her udder hidden by an apron so as not to offend.

Mickey Mouse was banned in Romania in 1935 because they thought he would scare young children.

NO BODY'S PERFECT

Demi Moore was cross-eyed as a kid and needed two surgeries to straighten things out.

Jane Seymour's left eye is green and the right one is brown.

Jean Harlow didn't wear bras in her movies. To emphasize this fact, she would rub ice on her nipples before filming, to decided effect.

OCCUPATIONAL HAZARDS

Clark Gable's ears were so big and floppy that he had trouble getting roles early in his career. He eventually had plastic surgery and taped them back while filming.

Supposedly, Clark Gable's breath was so bad that Vivien Leigh gagged while kissing him on the set of *Gone with the Wind*.

Clint Eastwood took a mid-career break from making Westerns because he became allergic to horses.

It is said that Katharine Hepburn had such a phobia about dirty hair that she went around the movie sets smelling people's hair.

SOME LIKE IT HOT

Marilyn Monroe lived in a long line of foster homes as a child and married at the age of sixteen to avoid being shipped off to another.

During the filming of *Some Like It Hot*, Marilyn's costar Tony Curtis quipped that their love scenes were "like kissing Hitler."

Marilyn Monroe never wore panties, either on or off the set. She also bleached her pubic hair, slept in the nude, ate in bed, and had irritable bowel syndrome.

The dress Marilyn wore to sing "Happy Birthday, Mr. President" to John F. Kennedy in Madison Square Garden was so sheer and tight-fitting that she wore nothing under it and literally had to be sewn into it.

Marilyn was often tardy, and this was the case the night she serenaded the president. The show's host, Peter Lawford, introduced her as "the late Marilyn Monroe." She died three months later.

After Marilyn's death, Shirley MacLaine took her roles in two upcoming movies.

LIFE IMITATES ART

A psychiatric condition known as "Truman Syndrome," where some people are convinced that their whole life is part of a reality show that is secretly being taped, was named after the Jim Carrey movie *The Truman Show*.

LONG LIVE ROCK

OPENING NOTES

The first ever musical audio recording was made by Thomas Edison in 1877 of "Mary Had a Little Lamb."

Early records were played at 78 rotations per minute (rpm) because the phonographs had to be hand-cranked and that number closely matched the number of heartbeats per minute.

The cassette tape was introduced in 1963.

The compact disc became available in the United States in 1983. Five years later, CDs outsold vinyl records.

The last eight-track tape released by a major label was *Fleetwood Mac's Greatest Hits* in 1988.

The portable MP3 player hit the market in 1997.

IT'S STILL ROCK 'N' ROLL TO ME

Three songs in the 1940s had the words "rock and roll" in their titles. It was disc jockey Alan Freed who first used the term to describe this genre of music in 1951.

When Decca Records released *Rock Around the Clock*, by Bill Haley and His Comets, in 1954, most people had never heard of rock 'n' roll, so the company put a label on the single describing it as a "Novelty Foxtrot."

STICKY FINGERS

The Rolling Stones *Sticky Fingers* album cover features an Andy Warhol photograph of the large crotch bulge of gay subculture star Joe Dallesandro's tight jeans, complete with working zipper. It was named the number one album cover of all time by VH-1. The album also first featured the iconic "Tongue and Lip Design," which was recently voted the greatest rock logo of all time.

In 1969, Mick Jagger was quoted as saying, "I don't really like singing very much. I enjoy playing the guitar more than I enjoy singing, and I can't play the guitar either."

The Rolling Stones have had four of the top ten highest grossing North American tours since 1985.

The Rolling Stones name comes from the 1950 Muddy Waters song "Rollin' Stone."

Keith Richards admitted to mixing his dead father's ashes with cocaine and snorting him.

SHOOTING STARS

Terry Kath, the original guitarist for Chicago, died in 1978, after putting a 9mm pistol to his head and pulling the trigger. He apparently showed a friend an empty clip first and said, "Don't worry, it's not loaded." Alas, one bullet remained in the magazine.

In 1971, guitarist Duane Allman crashed his motorcycle into the back of a truck in Macon, Georgia. His bandmate, bassist Berry Oakley, was killed when he crashed his motorcycle into a city bus just three blocks away, a year later.

"Mama" Cass Elliot died in the same London apartment, in 1974, which Keith Moon would die in four years later.

Brad Delp, a founding member of the group Boston, committed suicide by taking two charcoal grills into a sealed bathroom.

THE KING IS DEAD

Elvis died sitting on the toilet reading *The Scientific Search for Jesus*.

Graceland is the second most visited home in America, after the White House.

THERE IS NO DARK SIDE OF THE MOON

If the Pink Floyd album *Dark Side of the Moon* is started just as the MGM lion roars for the third time at the beginning of *The Wizard of Oz*, some strange synchronicities between the album and film will occur. In 2000, Turner Movie Classics (TCM) played the movie along with the album as a soundtrack.

Dark Side of the Moon stayed on the Billboard album charts for a record 725 weeks.

On the *Dark Side of the Moon* song "Brain Damage," the band's road manager—Peter Watts (actress Naomi's father)—did the weird laughter in the background.

Paul McCartney's Wings bandmate Henry McCullough did the "I was really drunk at the time" line between "Money" and "Us and Them."

Pink Floyd used to be called the Tea Set, before naming themselves the Pink Floyd Sound, after two Piedmont bluesmen—Pink Andersen and Floyd Council.

All Pink Floyd's founding members, except Syd Barrett, met while studying architecture at London's Regent Polytechnic Institute in 1964.

The single "Another Brick in the Wall" was banned by the BBC in 1980, while going to number one in the United States.

BAD MOON RISING

Keith Moon joined the Who after telling Roger Daltrey, during a show, that he could play better than the drummer they had.

The Who would banish Keith Moon from the studio while recording the vocals because his singing was so bad.

Keith Moon was infamous for trashing hotel rooms. He blew up $500,000 worth of toilets with cherry bombs, M-80s, and dynamite, getting him banned for life from all Holiday Inns, Sheratons, and Hilton Hotels world wide. He once drove his Cadillac into a swimming pool in Flint, Michigan.

In 1970, Keith Moon accidentally ran over and killed his friend and bodyguard Neil Boland with his Bentley.

During a 1973 show, Keith Moon passed out twice from large quantities of alcohol and tranquilizers. Quick-thinking Pete Townshend asked the crowd if anyone could play the drums and used an audience member to finish the gig.

Keith Moon died of a massive sedative overdose, three weeks after the release of the *Who Are You* LP. Ironically, on the album cover photo, he is seated in a chair labeled "NOT TO BE TAKEN AWAY."

The Who's present drummer is Zak Starkey, Ringo Starr's son, whom Keith Moon taught how to play.

The character of Animal on *The Muppet Show* was based on Keith Moon.

WE GOT THE BEAT

Andy White, the drummer on the Beatles song "Love Me Do," was only ever paid the original session fee of seven pounds (around fourteen dollars).

Paul McCartney plays drums on "Dear Prudence" and "Back in the U.S.S.R." because Ringo Starr had walked out on the recordings.

ODD OPENING ACTS

Jimi Hendrix was the opening act for the Monkees in 1967. Monkees fans booed him off the stage and he quit the tour after two weeks.

Bruce Springsteen and the E Street Band once opened for Anne Murray of "Snowbird" fame.

SHARP-DRESSED MEN

ZZ Top guitarist Billy Gibbons has said their name honors B. B. King. At first they wanted to be Z. Z. King, but that was too similar to their hero's name, so they settled on "Top" because King was tops with them. (Others suggest the name comes from two brands of rolling papers—Zig-Zag and Top.)

Billy Gibbons does the spoken lyrics between each verse in the 2005 Nickelback song "Rockstar."

PURPLE HAZE

Jimi Hendrix was left-handed and played a right-hand guitar, turned upside down and restrung with the heavier strings in their normal position at the top of the neck.

Hendrix was fired between sets from his first gig with a band playing in a synagogue basement, for being too wild.

Although he taught himself to play guitar, Jimi got an F in high school music class.

At nineteen, Hendrix got into trouble with the law and was given the choice to join the army or go to jail. He chose the former, but was discharged after a year for being a slacker.

BEASTIES

According to Michael Diamond (aka Mike D) of the Beastie Boys, *Beastie* is an acronym for Boys Entering Anarchistic Stages Towards Internal Excellence.

The Beastie Boys's 1986 album *Licensed to Ill* was the first rap album to go to number one on the Billboard charts.

PRINCE OF DARKNESS

In 1981, Ozzy Osbourne bit the head off a live dove at a record company meeting. A few months later, he bit the head off a bat that had been thrown onto the stage by a fan. Ozzy claimed he thought it was a rubber bat, but he had to endure a series of rabies shots after the incident.

Ozzy and fellow Black Sabbath member drummer Bill Ward dropped acid every day for two years.

In 1982, a small plane carrying members of Ozzy's entourage was buzzing Ozzy's tour bus outside Orlando, Florida. The plane's wing clipped the bus and crashed, killing his guitarist and hairdresser, among others.

During the late 1980s, Ozzy was sued three times by families claiming his song "Suicide Solution" made their kids kill themselves. The song, which is supposedly about deceased AC/DC singer Bon Scott, is actually anti-suicide. Ozzy won each case.

In 1982, Ozzy was banned for ten years from the city of San Antonio, Texas, after being arrested drunk at 11:30 a.m., for urinating on the Alamo while wearing future wife Sharon's dress. Ozzy has also been banned, for various reasons, from Baton Rouge, Boston, Corpus Christi, Las Vegas, and Philadelphia.

ROCK 'N' ROLL ALL NIGHT . . .

The band KISS started out with the name Wicked Lester.

The first public performance by KISS drew three people.

KISS had to change the band's logo for the German market, where representations of the Nazi SS insignia are illegal.

Gene Simmons's real name is Chaim Witz.

Paul Stanley's real name is Stanley Harvey Eisen.

WHO ARE YOU?

The Who are said to have come by their name when one day while taking suggestions, someone noticed that they were already so hard of hearing they kept saying "the who?"

The traditional story behind the Led Zeppelin name has it that Who members John Entwistle and Keith Moon said a band composed of them with Jeff Beck and Jimmy Page would go over like a "lead zeppelin." Page formed the band without the other three and dropped the "a" from "lead" because his manager thought "thick Americans" would mispronounce it "leed."

The Ramones were named to honor Paul McCartney, who went by the name Paul Ramone during his Silver Beatles days. All the members of the band used this last name.

UB40 got their name from the British unemployment benefit form UB40.

Steely Dan is named for "Steely Dan III from Yokahoma," a dildo in William Burroughs's 1959 novel *Naked Lunch*. Founders Donald Fagen and Walter Becker were both avid readers of 1950s Beat literature.

The band Rush was rushing to think up a name before their first gig, when John Rutsey's older brother yelled, "Why don't you call your band Rush?"

Queen got its name for obvious reasons—Freddie Mercury liked the transvestite inference and also thought queens and royalty were glamorous.

The Eagles were originally called Teen King and the Emergencies. Glenn Frey was nicknamed "Teen King" because he scored with all the ladies. They chose the Eagles in honor of the Byrds.

Devo is short for de-evolution, or regression, which is what the band thought the world was going through.

The Backstreet Boys used to hang out at the Backstreet Market, an Orlando flea market.

Foo Fighters was the name for strange unidentified flying objects that World War II pilots sometimes saw.

Marshall Mathers combined his initials—*M* and *M*—and spelled them phonetically to come up with Eminem.

Limp Bizkit comes from Fred Durst's dog Biscuit, which had a limp.

David Bowie used to be David Jones, but renamed himself after the knife, in order to avoid being confused with Davy Jones of the Monkees.

The name Simple Minds is from a line in the David Bowie song "Jean Genie."

The name Toad the Wet Sprocket was from Eric Idle's monologue "Rock Notes," on Monty Python's 1980 *Contractual Obligation* album.

The Mothers of Invention began as the Mothers (short for mother f——ers), but their record label persuaded them to add "of Invention."

Judas Priest is taken from the Bob Dylan song "The Ballad of Frankie Lee and Judas Priest."

Robert Allen Zimmerman became Robert Allen and then Bob Dylan in honor of Welsh poet Dylan Thomas.

Jerry Garcia found the name Grateful Dead while smoking a psychedelic drug and browsing through Funk & Wagnalls' *Standard Dictionary of Folklore, Mythology, and Legend*. The term describes a spirit who is thankful to someone who arranged for burial of the spirit's physical form as an act of charity. (They were first called Warlocks, but that name was already taken by another band.)

Grand Funk Railroad, later just Grand Funk, was inspired by Michigan's Grand Trunk Western Railroad.

The name Bad Company is from a 1972 Jeff Bridges movie of the same name.

AC/DC came from a sewing machine label. The band knew it meant electric, but didn't know about the bisexual connotations.

The Bay City Rollers came up with their moniker by throwing a dart at a map, which landed on Bay City, Michigan.

Paul Hewson picked up the alias "Bono" from the name of a hearing aid store in Dublin called "Bono Vox." A friend used to joke that Hewson sang so loud it was like he was singing for the deaf.

Blue Oyster Cult was known as Soft White Underbelly until they received a bad review and wanted a new identity. They went through several names before their manager hit on Blue Oyster Cult, from a poem he had written about a collection of aliens who gathered to guide Earth's history.

Buffalo Springfield was the name of an asphalt-rolling machine parked outside a home the band was staying in.

Deep Purple was the name of an old hit song that Ritchie Blackmore's grandma loved and wanted him to perform on stage.

Dire Straits described the financial condition of the band when they first got started.

BEHIND THE HITS

Songwriter David Ritz commented that Marvin Gaye needed some "sexual healing" after seeing Gaye's large pornography collection. The two then collaborated on the hit song.

"Unchained Melody" by the Righteous Brothers was originally released as the B-side of the single "Hung on You." Luckily, some DJs turned it over for a listen.

Two hits by Jim Croce were about real people. "You Don't Mess Around with Jim" was about Jim Walker, "a pool shootin' son of a gun" from south Philly. "Leroy Brown" was a fellow member of Croce's Air National Guard unit who went AWOL.

There really was a girl named Jenny, whose parents' phone number was 867-5309.

"Jeremiah was a bullfrog" was just a filler line songwriter Hoyt Axton used when writing "Joy to the World," until he could think of better lyrics. Three Dog Night liked it that way and left it in.

LINER NOTES

Left-handed heavy metal guitar legend Tony Iommi accidentally cut off the tips of the middle and ring fingers of his right hand on the last day of his job at a sheet metal factory, when he was seventeen. He tried learning to strum right-handed, but ended up using the lightest strings he could find (banjo strings) and wearing plastic tips he made for himself on his fingers.

Van Halen had a stipulation in their concert contracts that a bowl of M&M's be provided in their dressing room with all the brown ones removed. They once trashed a dressing room after this demand wasn't met.

United Artists titled Electric Light Orchestra's debut album *No Answer*, after a company representative phoned the band to find out what the LP should be called, got no answer, and jotted the two words down. The phrase was then mistaken for the title.

Robin Gibb of the Bee Gees, the group that wrote and performed most of the soundtrack for the movie *Saturday Night Fever*, says he has never seen the movie all the way through.

Jimmy Buffett's first album sold 324 copies.

Eric Clapton studied stained glass design as a teen.

ARTS AND LETTERS

BESTSELLERS

Less than 1 percent of all books published sell fifty thousand or more copies.

The bestselling novel of all time is Charles Dickens's *Tale of Two Cities*, which has sold roughly 200 million copies. *The Lord of the Rings*, by J.R.R. Tolkien, has sold some 150 million.

Catch-22 never appeared on a bestseller list

Moby Dick sold less than ten thousand copies in Herman Melville's lifetime.

Washington Irving was the first American to make a living solely from writing.

USA Today is the number one daily newspaper in the United States, with a circulation of 2.5 million.

Reader's Digest has the world's largest consumer magazine circulation.

OLDIES BUT GOODIES

The oldest continuously published newspaper is the Dutch paper *Haarlems Dagblad*, which debuted in 1656.

Scientific American has been published since 1845, longer than any other American magazine.

FRANKLY MY DEAR . . .

Gone with the Wind was the only book Margaret Mitchell had published in her lifetime. Another manuscript was found by an old lover's son and published as the novella *Lost Laysen* in 1996. Mitchell had written it when she was fifteen.

Margaret Mitchell originally wanted the title of *Gone with the Wind* to be *Tomorrow Is Another Day* or *Tote the Weary Load*.

Scarlett was originally named Pansy.

MOST PRECOCIOUS

The youngest published author is Dorothy Straight of Virginia, who wrote *How the World Began* (Pantheon, 1964) when she was just four years old.

NOT EXACTLY MOTHER GOOSE

The earliest version of the "Sleeping Beauty" story was published in 1531 and involved the girl being raped and giving birth while still asleep.

UPSTANDING WRITERS

Lewis Carroll, Winston Churchill, Charles Dickens, Ernest Hemingway, Thomas Jefferson, and George Sand all wrote standing up.

THE BARD OF AVON

Shakespeare has been credited with adding scores of sayings to the English language, including:

A horse, a horse! My kingdom for a horse! (*Richard III*)

All that glitters is not gold. (*The Merchant of Venice*)

All the world's a stage. (*As You Like It*)

A pound of flesh. (*The Merchant of Venice*)

A sorry sight. (*Macbeth*)

A spotless reputation. (*Richard II*)

Bated breath. (*The Merchant of Venice*)

Brave new world. (*The Tempest*)

Budge an inch. (*The Taming of the Shrew*)

Eaten me out of house and home. (*Henry IV*)

Foregone conclusion. (*Othello*)

For goodness' sake. (*Henry VII*)

Full circle. (*King Lear*)

Heart on my sleeve. (*Othello*)

In my heart of hearts. (*Hamlet*)

In my mind's eye. (*Hamlet*)

Knock, knock! Who's there? (*Macbeth*)

Let's kill all the lawyers. (*Henry VI*)

Method in the madness. (*Hamlet*)

Neither a borrower, nor a lender be. (*Hamlet*)

Neither rhyme, nor reason. (*The Comedy of Errors*)

Parting is such sweet sorrow. (*Romeo and Juliet*)

Pomp and circumstance. (*Othello*)

Short shrift. (*Richard III*)

Something is rotten in the state of Denmark. (*Hamlet*)

Strange bedfellows. (*The Tempest*)

Sweets to the sweet. (*Hamlet*)

The be all and end all. (*Macbeth*)

The better part of valor is discretion. (*Henry IV*)

The green-eyed monster. (*Othello*)

The milk of human kindness. (*Macbeth*)

The most unkindest cut of all. (*Julius Caesar*)

The primrose path. (*Hamlet*)

Too much of a good thing. (*As You Like It*)

To thine own self be true. (*Hamlet*)

Uneasy lies the head that wears the crown. (*Henry IV*)

What's done is done. (*Macbeth*)

CAT IN THE HAT

Theodor Seuss Geisel dropped out of Oxford graduate school before getting his PhD, so he called himself "Dr." Seuss as a nod to his disappointed father.

Dr. Seuss was turned down by twenty-seven publishers before selling his first book.

The Cat in the Hat took one and a half years to write and illustrate.

WHAT WERE THEY THINKING?

J. K. Rowling was turned down by twelve publishers.

Some of the books banned in the United States over the years include *The Adventures of Huckleberry Finn, The Grapes of Wrath, Little Red Riding Hood, The Merchant of Venice, Tropic of Cancer,* and *Ulysses.*

Mario Puzo received a mere five-thousand-dollar advance for *The Godfather*, as did Tom Clancy for *The Hunt for Red October*.

At the other end of the spectrum, *Cold Mountain* author Charles Frazier got $8.25 million for writing *Thirteen Moons* in 2006. Only about half of the 750,000 books in the first print run were sold. Random House lost around $5.5 million on the advance.

STRIP SEARCH

Snoopy was based on *Peanuts* creator Charles Schulz's dog Spike. Schulz had planned to name the cartoon dog "Sniffy," until he found out another comic strip had a dog with that name. Snoopy's desert-dwelling brother is named Spike.

The Katzenjammer Kids comic strip has been running since 1897.

ENDNOTES

The longest book in the Bible is Psalms. The shortest is II John.

Only 0.3 cents of every dollar spent in America goes for reading materials.

WHAT DO YOU MEAN?

A contranym is a word that has opposite meanings, for example:

"Sanction" can mean approve or punishment.

"Clip" can mean cut or fasten.

"Cleave" can mean split apart or join together.

"Screen" can mean shield or present.

"Trim" can mean to cut away or to ornament.

WHAT I MEANT TO SAY . . .

While giving a 1977 speech in Poland, President Jimmy Carter wanted to say in Polish that he wished to understand the Poles' desires for the future and that he liked the Poles. What he said came out, in translation, as "I desire Poles carnally."

Pepsi-Cola's "Come alive with Pepsi" was translated as "Come alive out of the grave" in Germany.

ALPHABET SOUP

The English language has about 600,000 words, according to the Oxford Dictionary.

English is the official or predominately spoken language in sixty countries.

The ten most common written words in the English language are "the, of, and, a, in, to, is, as, it, for." One in every sixteen words is "the."

The ten most common spoken English words are "be, the, I, you, and, it, have, a, do, not."

The word "set" has 464 definitions in the Oxford English Dictionary.

ABCS

The Solomon Island alphabet has eleven letters.

The Welsh alphabet contains twenty-eight letters, but no J, K, Q, V, X, or Z. Eight of the characters are digraphs, or a pair of letters representing a sound: CH, DD, FF, NG, LL, PH, RH, and TH.

WORD WISE

In Hebrew, *nasa* means "to go up."

The word "Boston" is believed to be a contraction of "Botolph's Tun," a town in Lincolnshire, England, founded by a Saxon monk in 654 CE. Some of the Pilgrims were imprisoned there in 1607.

Umbrellas were invented to block the sun, not the rain. *Umbra* is Latin for "shadow."

"In the buff" came to mean "naked" in the seventeenth century because English soldiers' tunics, or "buffs," had a similar color to the British backside.

The word "sex" didn't come to mean sexual intercourse until D. H. Lawrence used it in that context in a 1929 novel.

The Mosquito Coast in Honduras and Nicaragua is

not named for the insect, but is a misspelling of the name of the Miskito Indians who live there.

On Thanksgiving Day 1904, the Salvation Army used New York City's water wagons to collect drunks off the streets of the Bowery and put them "on the wagon" in hopes of drying them out—hence, the expression.

Mazda is named for the Persian god of light—Ahura Mazda.

The word "okay" is likely from the 1840 reelection campaign of Martin Van Buren, who had the nickname "Old Kinderhook," after his birthplace in New York State. His supporters formed the "OK Club."

"Limey" became a derogatory name for the English when their navy switched from costly lemon juice to the cheaper lime juice to prevent scurvy. The disease returned, and American and Australian sailors made fun of the afflicted "Limeys."

A toilet is called a "john" after Englishman John Harrington, who devised the first flush toilet at the end of the 1500s.

In Middle English, the word *pygg* was a type of clay used to fashion jars. People kept coins in the jars, and over time this practice led to the modern piggy bank.

The word "noon" is from the Latin *nona hora*, meaning "ninth hour," referring to the ninth hour after sunrise, or

3 p.m. In English, the meaning changed to "midday" by around 1100 CE.

"Salmonella" is named for Daniel Elmer Salmon, who first described it in 1885.

The word "pound" comes from the Latin *pendere*, meaning "to weigh."

The word "dime" comes from the Latin *decem*, meaning "ten."

Coins minted from the sixteenth-century Joachimsthal silver mine in Bohemia came to be called "thalers." From this the word "dollar" arose.

Governor Elbridge Gerry of Massachusetts had an electoral district redrawn to benefit his party in 1812. The shape of the district was so "tortuous" that it was said to look like a "salamander." The *Boston Gazette* ran a cartoon of the district drawn as a mythical beast—the "Gerrymander."

YES, VIRGINIA . . .

There really was a "Sally" who sold seashells by the seashore. A young teen named Mary Anning discovered the fossil remains of an ancient sea creature on the English coast around 1812. She went on to become perhaps the most astute fossil collector of all time and made a living selling fossils and shells to tourists. A man named Terry Sullivan wrote the tongue twister about her fifty years after her death.

Little Miss Muffet was the daughter of a sixteenth-century naturalist, Dr. Thomas Muffet, who studied, you guessed it—spiders. (A tuffet, in case you were wondering, is a large cushion used as a seat or footstool.)

A girl named Mary Sawyer had a little lamb that she took to school one day in 1830, causing quite a stir. Sarah Josepha Hale is credited with writing the poem commemorating the event. Mary's house, in Sterling, Massachusetts, burned down in 2007, but the old Redstone Schoolhouse still exists, in Sudbury, Massachusetts.

GOD OF THE MONTH

January is named for the Roman god Janus, who had two heads, one facing backward to look at the old year, and one facing forward to look at the new.

February is named for the Roman purification festival, Februa, the last month of the Roman year.

March is named for the Roman god of war and agriculture—Mars.

April is from the Latin *aperire*, which means "to open." This is the time of year flower and leaf buds open.

May is named for the Greek goddess of fertility—Maia.

June is named for the Roman goddess of marriage—Juno. It was thought lucky to be married in June.

July is named for Julius Caesar, who was born in this month.

August was named for Augustus Caesar, who defeated Mark Antony and Cleopatra on August 1, 30 BCE.

September, October, November, and December are named for the Latin words meaning seventh (*septem*), eighth (*octo*), ninth (*novem*), and tenth (*decem*), respectively. They were the seventh, eighth, ninth, and tenth months of the Roman calendar.

DAY BY DAY

Sunday derives from the Old English *sunnandaeg*, meaning "day of the sun."

Monday is from the Old English *monandaeg*, or "day of the moon."

Tuesday is from the Old English *tiwesdaeg*, for the Norse god of combat.

Wednesday is from *wodnesdaeg*, after the supreme Norse god Woden.

Thursday is from *thorsdaeg*, after the Norse god of thunder, Thor.

Friday is from *frigedaeg*, after Frige, the Norse goddess of beauty, wife of Woden.

Saturday is the only day to retain its Roman origin, named after Saturn, god of agriculture and harvest.

P.S.

Habseligkeiten, meaning "belongings," was selected by the German Language Council as the most beautiful sounding word in the language. (A word only a German could love.)

Henry VIII was the first king to be called Your "Majesty."

Middle names were uncommon in America until the eighteenth century.

The last word in many dictionaries is "zyzzyva," a tropical weevil.

. . . I KNOW WHAT I LIKE

Pablo Picasso was questioned in connection with the theft of the *Mona Lisa* from the Louvre in 1911, but released.

Las Vegas casino magnate Steve Wynn put his elbow through the canvas of a Pablo Picasso painting that he had arranged to sell for $139 million in 2006. His clumsiness killed the deal. Whoops!

The famous twelve-by-twenty-one-foot picture *Washington Crossing the Delaware* was painted in Germany by Emanuel Leutze and was modeled on the Rhine. This is why there are huge chunks of ice floating around the boats, something not seen in the Delaware. The American flag in the boat was not created until well after Washington's crossing and the boats are far too small to have transported Washington's men.

The painting *La Beteau*, by Henri Matisse, hung upside down for forty-seven days in the Metropolitan Museum of Art in New York before anyone noticed.

During the last seventy days of his life, Van Gogh completed seventy paintings.

Jackson Pollock's 1948 painting *No. 5* sold for a record $140 million in 2006.

The State Hermitage Museum in St. Petersburg, Russia, is the largest art museum in the world, with 322 galleries and more than 3 million pieces of art.

Red, White, and Blue

AMERICA THE BEAUTIFUL

Steamboat Geyser in Yellowstone National Park shoots water up to one thousand feet in the air.

The longest cave in the world is Mammoth Cave in Kentucky, which is around 350 miles in length.

Niagara Falls, while not the tallest or largest, is the waterfall with the greatest mean annual flow of water.

The deepest lake in the United States is Oregon's Crater Lake at 1,949 feet.

ELBOW ROOM

New Jersey is the most densely populated state, with 1,134 residents per square mile. Yet 37 percent of New Jersey—the Garden State—is forested.

Alaska is the most sparsely populated state, with only one person per square mile.

The King Ranch in Texas is bigger than the state of Rhode Island.

Juneau, Alaska, is almost as big as Rhode Island and Delaware combined.

IN GOOD HANDS

New Jersey has the highest car insurance rates of any state, North Dakota the lowest.

The city with the highest auto insurance rates is Detroit. Roanoke, Virginia, is cheapest.

Texas has the highest homeowner insurance rates, followed by Louisiana. (Think hurricanes.)

The most dangerous states to work in are Alaska, Montana, North Dakota, and Wyoming (due to heavy agricultural activity). The safest are New Jersey, Connecticut, Rhode Island, Massachusetts, and New Hampshire.

North Dakota and Florida have the fewest earthquakes.

COME, ALL YE FAITHFUL

Holy Trinity (Old Swedes) Church in Wilmington, Delaware, which was established in 1698, is the oldest American Protestant church still in use.

Far more women attend regular weekend church services than do men—61 percent to 39 percent.

People in the South and Utah are the most frequent churchgoers.

Blacks attend church more often than whites.

Maryland was founded in 1634 as a Catholic colony.

🌰 DECK THE HALLS

The General Court of Massachusetts banned the celebration of Christmas in 1659. They thought it was pagan to hang decorations and fined those who did.

Christmas was made a national holiday in 1870.

The first person to put colored lights on a Christmas tree was Edward Johnson, an executive at Edison's electric company, who adorned the evergreen in his parlor with them in 1882. This created such a buzz that by 1890, Edison began selling the lights commercially.

STATE YOUR NAME

Pennsylvania is named for Admiral Penn, father of the Quaker William Penn, who was granted the land by Charles II in 1681. The name means "Penn's Woods."

Delaware was named for Lord De La Ware, an early governor of Virginia.

The District of Columbia was named for Christopher Columbus.

Georgia was named for King George II of England.

Louisiana was named for King Louis XIV of France.

Maryland was named for Queen Henrietta Maria, the wife of Charles I and mother of Charles II of England.

New York was named for the Duke of York, the brother of Charles II of England, who sent an expedition to capture it from the Dutch in 1664.

North and South Carolina's names are derived from the Latin for Charles (I)—*Carolus*.

Virginia was named by Sir Walter Raleigh, for Elizabeth I (the Virgin Queen).

Washington is named for George Washington.

One-half of all U.S. state names are derived from Native American words.

Nome, Alaska, is thought to be named after nearby Cape Nome, which may have gotten its odd name after a British naval officer didn't know what to call the area and made the notation "? Name" on his charts. A later mapmaker misread this as "C. Nome," or Cape Nome, and entered it on his map.

Washington Irving first used the nickname "Gotham," an Anglo-Saxon word meaning "goat's town," for New York City in 1807.

ALOHA STATE

Hawaii is the only state that has a royal residence—Iolani Palace, in Honolulu.

The tallest mountain in the world, measured from the base, is Mauna Kea on the Big Island of Hawaii. It rises 33,123 feet above the ocean floor.

Mauna Loa in Hawaii is the largest volcano in the world.

The state of Hawaii is comprised of hundreds of islands that stretch out for fifteen hundred miles.

Hawaii, California, New Mexico, and Texas are the only states where minorities outnumber white people.

SOUTHERN COMFORT

West Virginia was formed after Virginia seceded from the Union in 1861 and the western portion of the state seceded from Virginia. In 1863, West Virginia was admitted to the Union.

West Virginia was temporarily named Kanawha after it seceded from Virginia.

Virginia extends ninety-five miles farther west than West Virginia.

REPUBLIC OF VERMONT

Vermont declared itself an independent nation in 1777. It was admitted to the Union as a state in 1791.

> The Green Mountain Boys, of Fort Ticonderoga fame, were actually formed by the Republic of Vermont to fight against New York, which claimed the land as its own.

OH, SAY, CAN YOU SEE?

The original name of "The Star Spangled Banner" was "In Defence of Fort McHenry."

> "The Star Spangled Banner" was designated the American national anthem by Congress in 1931. It has four stanzas of thirty-two lines. We only sing the first stanza (eight lines).

There is no historical evidence that Betsy Ross sewed the first stars and stripes.

> The music for "My Country, 'Tis of Thee" is taken from "God Save the Queen/King." In 1831, a Baptist minister set the song to this music, not realizing that it was the British anthem.

OLD TOWN

St. Augustine, Florida, is the oldest permanent European settlement in what is now the United States. The Spanish ceded it to the United States in 1821.

OY, OYSTERS!

For more than three hundred years, Virginia and Maryland were involved in an interstate conflict known as the "Oyster Wars," fought over Virginia's right to harvest oysters from the Potomac River and Bay. The often bloody dispute wasn't finally resolved until compromise laws were passed in 1962.

BLUE AND GRAY

In 1864, during the Civil War, Admiral David Farragut was referring to the naval mines in the waters of Mobile Bay, not self-propelled torpedoes, when he yelled, "Damn the torpedoes, full speed ahead!"

It wasn't until 1870, five years after the Civil War, that all the Confederate states were readmitted to the Union.

HOME ON THE RANGE

Contrary to popular belief, wagon trains did not form circles as a defense from Indian attacks, but to form a corral for horses and as a shield from the elements.

Cahokia, a Native American urban center located in southern Illinois, is believed to have been the most populous city in what is now the United States until 1800, with a population that may have approached forty thousand.

GREENBACKS

The U.S. government first issued paper money, known as "greenbacks," in 1861, to help fund the Civil War.

The Bureau of Engraving and Printing—the guys who print U.S. currency—also print a wide variety of other certificates—from the one-fifth cent wine stamp to the $100 million International Monetary Fund special note.

Seventy-five million dollars of old money is shredded each day and used for insulation, roof shingles, fireplace logs, and fertilizer.

There are bits of ground-up old blue jeans in dollar bills. They appear as little blue hairs.

The U.S. five-dollar bill has an exact replica of the Lincoln Memorial on its obverse (back) side. If you look closely along the top of the memorial, you will find the names of twenty-six states.

Martha Washington is the only female to appear on the face of a U.S. currency note—the one-dollar silver certificate of 1806 and 1891.

According to the Federal Reserve, the average life of a note depends on its denomination:

$1—22 months

$5—16 months

$10—18 months

$20—2 years

$50—5 years

$100—8½ years

The U.S. Bureau of Engraving and Printing uses eighteen tons of ink a day.

You would have to double-fold a dollar bill four thousand times before it would tear.

The old car on the back of a ten dollar bill is not a Ford Model T, but a composite of several cars of the time made up by the designer.

It is against federal law to burn U.S. currency.

There is about $829 billion in circulation, two-thirds of it outside of the country.

Up until 1933, Americans could redeem their paper money for its value in gold.

🌰 LOOSE CHANGE

In early American colonial times, Britain forbade the colonies from producing their own coins. The Massachusetts Bay Colony got around this ban by minting coins just after the English Civil War in 1652, when there was no monarchy. They continued to do so for more than thirty years, using the date 1652 on all the coins, so they could claim all the coins were minted at a time when royal authority did not exist.

In 1787, the Continental Congress commissioned the first American coin—the Fugio penny. Designed by Benjamin Franklin, the front had a sun rising over a sundial and the motto "Mind Your Business."

Seven billion pennies are minted a year.

Modern pennies are 97.5 percent zinc.

It costs much more to mint new pennies than their face value.

The motto "In God We Trust" first appeared on U.S. coins in 1864, as a way to boost the country's morale during the Civil War. It wasn't added to paper money until 1957.

ECONOFACTS

There was no U.S. federal income tax before 1913.

Prior to 1955, U.S. personal income tax returns were due on March 15.

California's economy is so large, with a gross domestic product of $1.73 trillion in 2006, that if it were a country, it would rank tenth in the world.

The Secret Service began, in 1865, as an agency to fight counterfeiting, a job that it is still responsible for.

The Federal Reserve Bank of New York, not Fort Knox,

holds the largest gold reserves in the world, in a vault sitting on bedrock eighty-six feet below the city.

Diners Club was the first credit card, in 1950. It could only be used at certain restaurants and hotels and the balance had to be paid off every month.

The first revolving credit card, which could be paid off over time, was the BankAmericard in 1958. It later became VISA.

HAPPY NEW YEAR!

New Year's Eve was first celebrated in Times Square in 1904. Prior to this, New York's Trinity Church was the in place to ring in the New Year.

Times Square was known as Longacre Square before the Times Building, owned by the *New York Times*, opened there in 1904.

New York Times owner Alfred Ochs had the first ball lowered in Times Square at midnight, ringing in 1908.

THE FRIENDLY SKIES

The top two U.S. passenger carriers in 2006 were American and Southwest, in that order.

Hartsfield-Jackson Atlanta International Airport is the busiest in the United States, with 89 million passengers in 2007. Chicago's O'Hare is number two.

The worst year for scheduled U.S. airline deaths since 1985 was 1996, with 342 (this does not include the deaths on September 11, 2001).

During 2007 and 2008, there were no airline fatalities in the United States, even though some 1.5 billion passengers flew.

GOLDEN YEARS

The number of American men and the number of American women between the ages of 20 and 29 are about even. There are 92 men for every 100 women in the 55-to-64 age group, 84 men per 100 women in the 65-to-74 age group, and only 46 men per 100 women aged 85 and above.

There are about forty thousand people aged one hundred and above in the United States.

Of Americans who have reached their one hundredth birthday, 80 percent are women.

BRAGGING RIGHTS

Iowa is the leading egg producing state, with 14.25 billion a year. It also leads the nation in corn, soybean, and pig production, and is second in red meat.

Iowa has the most grade A farmland of any state.

Kansas grows the most wheat.

North Carolina grows the most tobacco, followed by Kentucky.

Texas grows the most cotton.

Texas is also the number one crude oil–producing state.

One-third of the potatoes grown in America come from Idaho.

The United States is the top corn-growing country.

Roughly 90 percent of toothpicks come from Maine.

OF CHIEF IMPORTANCE

The state that the most U.S. presidents have come from is Virginia, with nine.

The undergraduate college the most presidents have attended is Harvard, with five.

Harry Truman never graduated college.

John F. Kennedy was the only Catholic president.

Eleven presidents have been Episcopal and seven Presbyterian.

Ronald Reagan was the only divorced president. Nancy was his second wife.

It wasn't the bullet fired by Charles Guiteau that killed President James Garfield, but the infection he got from the manure-covered hands of the surgeons who treated him.

Presidents John Tyler, Millard Fillmore, Andrew Johnson, and Chester Arthur had no vice president.

Before the election of Barack Obama, Herbert Hoover's vice president, Charles Curtis, who was American Indian, had the distinction of being the minority achieving the highest rank in American government.

Teddy Roosevelt was the first president to travel abroad.

After Abe Lincoln's inauguration, he walked to a local hotel and had corned beef and cabbage and blackberry pie.

🌰 OBAMARAMA

Barack Obama's inaugural extravaganza cost $160 million.

Obama lost in the 2000 Illinois Democratic primary for the U.S. House of Representatives.

In the 2008 presidential election, Obama received just eight votes in King County, Texas.

Barack Obama and Laura Bush are smokers.

BLAH, BLAH, BLAH

The shortest presidential inaugural address was George Washington's of just 135 words in 1793.

William Henry Harrison delivered the longest inaugural address in 1841, which was 8,445 words and ran nearly two hours.

The only presidents not to use a speechwriter were Thomas Jefferson, John Adams, John Quincy Adams, James Madison, Abraham Lincoln, Grover Cleveland, Theodore Roosevelt, and Woodrow Wilson.

FOUR SCORE AND . . .

Lincoln's Gettysburg Address wasn't a hit at the time. Edward Everitt warmed up the crowd with a two-hour oration, before Lincoln's two-minute speech. After Lincoln spoke, there was just a smattering of applause.

Contrary to popular belief, the Gettysburg Address was written ahead of time in Washington, DC, and not on the back of an envelope while riding on the train to Gettysburg.

FIRST LADIES

Dolly Madison saved the original copies of the Declaration of Independence and the Constitution when the British burned the White House during the War of 1812.

Grover Cleveland's wife, Frances, was only twenty-one when he took office. Frances's daughter, Esther Cleveland, is the only child to have been born in the White House.

James Monroe's wife, Elizabeth, had the servants address her as "Your Majesty."

Julia Grant was cross-eyed and Ulysses liked her that way.

Harry Truman met his wife, Bess, when they were both young children.

Lucy Hayes was the first first lady to graduate college.

Helen Taft was responsible for the planting of the beautiful cherry trees around the Washington, DC, Tidal Basin in 1912.

Florence Harding is suspected by some of having murdered her husband.

Edith Wilson was a descendent of Pocahontas.

During the time of Woodrow Wilson's incapacitation, Edith was essentially acting president, bypassing the vice president.

Eleanor Roosevelt was already named Eleanor Roosevelt before she married FDR. She was a distant cousin to Franklin and a niece of Teddy Roosevelt.

Eleanor Roosevelt kept a loaded handgun in her purse.

Lady Bird Johnson led a campaign to plant wildflowers along America's highways.

GENTLEMEN'S CLUB

U.S. senators were not always elected by popular vote, but were chosen by state legislatures. The Seventeenth Amendment to the Constitution changed this in 1913.

One nineteenth-century senator—James Shields—represented three different states at different times—Illinois, Minnesota, and Missouri.

Robert Byrd of West Virginia has been a senator for more than fifty years.

Strom Thurmond was a senator from South Carolina for forty-eight years. He retired when he was one hundred, in 2003.

Wayne Morse, a senator from Oregon, once gave an uninterrupted speech on the Senate floor for twenty-two hours and twenty-six minutes.

Female U.S. senators didn't get their own restroom until 1992. Before this they used the tourists' ladies' room.

THE THIRD BRANCH

The U.S. Supreme Court was founded in 1790, but didn't get its own building till 1935.

FAIR-WEATHER FRIENDS

When it rains on Election Day, more Democrats stay home than Republicans. Likewise, during inclement weather the young are more likely to skip voting than the elderly.

IS THAT ONE COAT OR TWO?

It takes 570 gallons of paint to cover the White House.

FILTHY RICH

John D. Rockefeller was the richest person of all time. In today's dollars, his worth would be close to $190 billion.

Ted Turner is the largest private landowner, with some 2 million acres in the American West. That's larger than the state of Delaware. He also has the largest private herd of bison—forty thousand.

YOUR LOCAL UPDATE

Alaska and Hawaii have the same record high temperature—100°F. This is the lowest high of any state.

Hawaii's low temperature is 12°F and Alaska's is −80°F.

The itchiest U.S. cities in August are Oklahoma City, Dallas, and St. Louis (according to the makers of Cortaid and SDI/Weather Trends).

Florida has more tornadoes per square mile than any other state.

Florida gets one hundred times more UV light than Maine.

Cape Hatteras, North Carolina, is the "city" most likely to be hit by a tropical storm or hurricane.

Las Vegas is the least humid city in the United States. Forks, Washington, is the most humid.

Cheyenne, Wyoming, has the cleanest air of any U.S. city.

CATS AND DOGS

On July 4, 1956, Unionville, Maryland, got 1.23 inches of rain in one minute.

Alvin, Texas, received forty-three inches of rain in twenty-four hours during Tropical Storm Claudette in 1979.

New York City gets more rain than Seattle, but Seattle has more cloudy days.

GOIN' POSTAL

The "zip" in ZIP code stands for the Zone Improvement Plan implemented by the U.S. Post Office Department in 1963. The first number denotes one of ten geographical mail areas. The second and third numbers indicate a metropolitan area or regional center, and the last two digits signify a small area or town within the larger region. An additional four-digit code was added in 1983 to further pinpoint a location.

The first self-adhesive stamps used by the U.S. Postal Service, in 1974, did not stick properly and the adhesive discolored the stamps.

People have to be dead for ten years before they can be on a U.S. postage stamp. Presidents only have to wait a year.

In 1940, Booker T. Washington became the first African American to be on a U.S. postage stamp.

Due to increased email usage, 9 billion fewer pieces of mail were sent in 2008 than in the previous year.

The postmaster general earned more than $800,000 in 2008, more than twice as much as the president.

SAVED FOR POSTERITY

A Big Mac museum opened in North Huntington, Pennsylvania, in 2007. Some other weird museums include:

The Dirt Museum in Boston, Massachusetts

The Spam Museum in Austin, Minnesota

The Cockroach Hall of Fame Museum in Plano, Texas

The Britt Hobo Museum in Britt, Iowa

BUILD IT AND THEY WILL COME

The roadway on the Verrazano-Narrows Bridge between Brooklyn and Staten Island is twelve feet higher in the winter because its steel cables contract in cold weather.

The Lake Pontchartrain Causeway Bridge in Louisiana, at 23.87 miles, is the longest over water.

The biggest stone sculpture in the world is the carving of Jefferson Davis, Robert E. Lee, and Stonewall Jackson at Stone Mountain, Georgia. The mounted figures are more than 90 feet high and 190 feet wide.

KEEP OFF THE GRASS

Before the Civil War, few Americans had front lawns. They were promoted by the Garden Club of America, the U.S. Department of Agriculture, and the U.S. Golf Association, late in the nineteenth century.

Before the lawn mower was invented, sheep did the job.

The United States spends more on its lawns and golf

courses than most countries spend on their entire agricultural system. The majority of other countries don't even have a lawn care industry.

OLD SCHOOL

Many familiar universities had different names years ago. Here's a list of what some famous schools were once called:

Brown University was called Rhode Island College.

Caltech was Throop College of Technology.

Juilliard was the Institute of Musical Arts.

MIT began as Boston Tech.

UCLA had the unusual name California State Normal School at Los Angeles.

The oldest continuously operating public school in America is the Boston Latin School, which was founded in 1635.

Harvard, founded in 1636, was named for clergyman John Harvard.

Harvard University, with $28 billion, has more endowment money than any other school.

Phi Beta Kappa, the oldest college society with Greek letters, was formed by five students at the College of William and Mary in 1776.

Ohio State is the largest single-campus college in America.

Some 30 percent of American ninth-graders never graduate from high school.

Nebraska boasts the top high school graduation rate in the country. Nevada is dead last.

About 1.7 percent of American kids are home-schooled.

There are a lot of weird college scholarships. Some of the stranger ones are given for the following:

Being left-handed

Being very tall or short

Being good at duck calling

Writing an essay on how milk helped you in school (milk mustache scholar)

Skateboarding

Having the last name van Valkenburg or Gatling or Gatlin

Knowing a lot about the FBI

Making your own prom outfit out of duct tape

Having the best apple pie recipe

Writing an essay about the novel *The Fountainhead*

Planning to study parapsychology

SPEED BUMPS

Thirteen states have speed limits as high as 75 miles per hour.

Hawaii has the lowest top speed limit—60 miles per hour.

New Jersey and Oregon are the only states where it is illegal to pump your own gas. Oddly, New Jersey usually has among the cheapest gas in the country, even though it's pumped for you.

Only 63.5 percent of people in New Hampshire and Wyoming wear their seat belts. In Washington State, 96.3 percent do.

New Hampshire is the only state where adults do not have to wear a seat belt.

About 46,000 people are killed on American roads every year. That includes 6,200 pedestrians.

All U.S. interstates that run east and west are even-numbered and increase from south to north. Those running north and south are odd-numbered and increase from west to east. City bypasses have three digits.

Residents of New York, Maryland, and New Jersey have the longest commuting times to work. North Dakotans have the shortest.

FROM THE FOUR CORNERS

At the Four Corners Monument in the American Southwest, Arizona, New Mexico, Utah, and Colorado all touch at one point. If you stand on that spot, you are in four states simultaneously.

The first nationwide American trade union—the National Cooperative of Cordwainers—was founded in 1836. (A cordwainer, or cordovan, is a person who works with soft leather to make shoes.)

The five most common last names in the United States are Smith, Johnson, Williams, Jones, and Brown.

The largest charity in the United States is the United Way.

The top three countries for U.S. foreign adoptions are China, Guatemala, and Russia.

People from Michigan are called Michiganders.

In 1830, Philadelphia became the first American city to have a public water system.

Most Americans didn't brush their teeth until after World War II.

The oldest working lighthouse in the United States is one on Sandy Hook, New Jersey, which was built in 1764.

WHAT IN THE WORLD?

WATERED DOWN

Lake Baikal in Siberia contains 20 percent of all the aqueous freshwater in the world.

Two-thirds of Lake Baikal's seventeen hundred species are found nowhere else.

The Lake Baikal seal is the only freshwater seal in the world.

The Amazon River carries as much water as the next ten largest rivers combined.

There are as many described species of fish in the Amazon as there are in the entire Atlantic Ocean.

The Aral Sea, in Central Asia, was once the fourth largest lake in the world. Due to the diversion of the two rivers that feed it, for irrigation, it is now only 10 percent of its former size and has become three small lakes.

With a drop of 2,647 feet, the water plummeting from Angel Falls, in Venezuela, turns to mist and blows away before hitting the ground.

Lake Malawi in Africa has the most different fish species of any lake. Its cichlids are popular aquarium fish.

Nearly 99 percent of Egyptians live on about 4 percent of the land—near the Nile River and its delta.

The Red Sea is 4.2 percent salt, making it the saltiest sea. The average salt content of the oceans is 3.5 percent. The Dead Sea is nine times saltier, making it the saltiest lake.

The tides in the Bay of Fundy, between Maine and New Brunswick, can rise 47.5 feet from low tide to high.

The tides in the Mediterranean only differ by one foot between high and low tide.

The largest swimming pool in the world is at the Chilean resort of San Alfonso del Mar. It is a kilometer long, thirty-five meters deep, and the size of six thousand normal pools.

COLD HARD FACTS

About 20 percent of the Earth is permanently frozen.

Nearly 10 percent of the world's ice is in Greenland, where the ice cap is fourteen thousand feet thick.

The ice in Antarctica contains about 70 percent of the world's freshwater.

Antarctica is 98 percent snow-covered.

Antarctica is the highest continent.

It snows very little at the poles. Snowstorms there are usually just the wind blowing around already fallen snow.

Antarctica is considered a desert. It only snows a few inches a year there, but the snowpack is up to seven thousand feet thick

There are more than seventy lakes buried thousands of feet beneath the Antarctic glacial ice, one as big as Lake Ontario.

The world's largest free-floating object is the seventy-one-mile-long Antarctic iceberg B15A, which calved in 2000.

NUMBER ONES

Brazil is the biggest exporter of beef.

Argentina is the biggest consumer of beef. Each person eats about 141 pounds a year.

China is the number one rice- and wheat-growing country. It also catches the most fish.

WHAT IN THE WORLD? 89

Côte d'Ivoire grows around 40 percent of the world's cocoa beans. The Swiss eat the most chocolate candy of any nation—more than twenty pounds a year.

Spain is the top grower of olives and producer of olive oil.

HIGHS AND LOWS

San Marino (yes, it's a country) has the most doctors and nurses per capita in the world.

The most undernourished country is Eritrea, in Africa.

The countries with the highest birthrates are Democratic Republic of the Congo, Guinea-Bissau, and Liberia. Germany and Singapore have the lowest.

Swaziland has the lowest life expectancy in the world, at 31.99 years.

Singapore has the lowest infant mortality rate, Angola the highest.

Transparency International ranks Bangladesh and Chad as the most corrupt countries and Iceland as the least corrupt.

There are more Jews in the United States than in Israel.

Having a resident population of just over five hundred, and millions of tourists each year, Vatican City has the highest per capita crime rate of any country in the world.

Colombia has the highest per capita murder rate of any country.

Monaco is the most densely populated country, Mongolia the least.

In Qatar there are 184 men for every 100 women. In Estonia there are 119 women for every 100 men.

Hong Kong has 195 skyscrapers higher than five hundred feet. New York City has 186.

Finland, Denmark, Sweden, Norway, and the Netherlands (in order) drink the most coffee per capita.

Ecuador has the greatest area of its land protected of any country—38 percent.

RUN IT UP THE FLAGPOLE

Thirteen nations have crescent moons on their flags.

One country has a monocolor flag—Libya. It's all green.

MOTHER TONGUES

Chinese is the most spoken language in the world, followed by Spanish and English.

Classical Chinese had no punctuation marks.

There are many variant spoken Chinese languages and hundreds of dialects. Fortunately, there is only one written Chinese language, so everyone can communicate.

There are about seven thousand dialects spoken around the world and about twelve are lost forever each year.

There are more than one thousand languages spoken in Africa.

Half of the world's countries have an official language. The United States does not.

India has fifteen official languages.

There is no word for "please" in Hindu.

In Turkish, there is no word to differentiate between "her," "him," and "it."

WORLD OF WONDER

Africa is the continent with the most countries.

The biggest exposed rock is the five-mile-long-by-two-mile-wide Mount Augustus in Australia. It is twice as big as the more famous Ayers Rock.

One-third of the land on Earth is desert.

Only 15 percent of the Sahara Desert is covered with sand; 70 percent is stones and gravel, and the rest, limestone and shale plateaus.

The Sahara is the biggest source of dust in the world.

Dust blown across the Atlantic from the Sahara can cause overcast skies in the Caribbean.

The Haskell Free Library and Opera House, in Stanstead, Quebec, and Derby Line, Vermont, straddles the U.S.-Canadian border. The front door is in Vermont and the back door is in Canada.

The country with the lowest elevation is the Maldives, where the highest point is only 7.8 feet.

China and Russia both border on fourteen other countries.

The largest patch of sand in the world is in the Texas-size "Empty Quarter" of the Arabian Peninsula.

The biggest ranch in the world is Anna Creek Station in Australia, which is larger than Israel. Due to a prolonged drought, the station only has three thousand head of cattle.

The Baltoro Glacier in Pakistan's Karakoram Range is the world's largest, at thirty-nine miles long and three miles wide.

HIGH AND DRY

The driest place in the world is Arica, Chile, where it only rains one day every six years.

Yuma, Arizona, is the sunniest place in the world. Phoenix is second.

NUKE 'EM

The United States, France, and Japan are the top three countries using nuclear reactors to make electricity.

France gets 78 percent of its electricity from nuclear power. It has fifty-six reactors and is the world's largest exporter of electricity.

Lithuania gets about 80 percent of its electricity from nukes.

MUCHO DINERO

The first ATM was installed at a Barclays Bank in Enfield, England, in 1967.

The island of Yap, in Micronesia, still recognizes giant stone discs as legal currency. Some are as large as twelve feet across.

In 1996, 75 percent of the workforce in Bosnia-Herzegovina was unemployed.

Denmark has a tax burden of 48.4 percent, the highest in the world, just ahead of Sweden.

Bahrain, Dubai, and Qatar have no personal income taxes.

Muslim Sharia law forbids the paying or charging of interest on loans.

The worst inflation ever occurred in post-WWII Hungary, in July 1946, when the rate of inflation was a mind-numbing 41,900,000,000,000,000 percent—the equivalent of prices doubling every thirteen and a half hours!

The largest banknote ever issued was the 1946 Hungarian 100 quintillion pengo note. That's a ten with twenty zeros.

Moscow has the highest cost of living in the world.

Workers in Austria and Portugal are entitled by law to thirty-five paid days off a year. Denmark, Finland, Germany, and Spain are right behind with thirty-four. Alas, Americans are guaranteed none.

One-half of the world's rough-cut diamonds pass through Israel's Diamond Exchange.

Japan has one vending machine for every twenty people and they can be found everywhere. Things you can get from a vending machine there include rice, pornography, a cell phone recharge, toilet paper, flowers, liquor, pet rhinoceros beetles, and used schoolgirl panties.

In Finland, speeding fines are based on a percentage of the driver's income.

ROYAL REIGNS

The Japanese imperial family goes back to the first emperor—Jimmu—circa 660 BCE.

> The shortest reign of any monarch was that of Crown Prince Luis Felipe of Spain, who was king for twenty minutes before dying in 1908. Assassins shot both him and his father, King Alfonso XII. The prince outlived his father briefly and was technically king during this time.

Conversely, Pepi II of Egypt ruled for ninety-four years, before dying in 2184 BCE.

🌰 CRAZY RICH

The Sultan of Brunei has a fleet of more than five hundred Rolls-Royces. He accounted for more than 50 percent of all Rolls-Royces sold in the 1990s. His car collection totals five thousand vehicles, for which he has paid an estimated $4 billion.

The Sultan's palace has 1,788 rooms, with 257 bathrooms, and encompasses more than 2,152,000 square feet.

RULE BRITANNIA

At the start of World War I, the British Empire encompassed one-fifth of the world and 25 percent of its people.

> During World War I, the British royal family name was changed from the Germanic Saxe-Coburg and Gotha, to the more English-sounding Windsor, for obvious PR reasons. The Battenberg family, likewise, changed their name to the less Germanic Mountbatten at the same time, at the request of King George V.

Mohammed is now the second most popular boys' first name in Britain, right behind Jack.

> When Britain withdrew from the Indian subcontinent in 1947, it was divided into Muslim Pakistan and Hindu India.

HIGHER POWERS

The oldest existing church is thought to be a brick-and-mud structure in Jordan from around 300 CE.

> The Basilica of Our Lady of Peace in Côte d'Ivoire is the largest church in the world.

In 1054, Pope Leo IX in Rome and Patriarch Michael Cerulrius in Constantinople excommunicated each other, forming the Roman Catholic Church and the Greek Orthodox Church. Several attempts at reconciliation have failed.

In Saudi Arabia, Friday is the day of prayer, so Thursday and Friday are the weekend.

Jain Dharma monks in India don't bathe any parts of their bodies except the hands and feet, believing doing so would kill countless millions of microbes.

NOTES FROM ABROAD

The Bang Na elevated expressway in Thailand, at 33.5 miles, is the longest bridge over land.

Cuba banned toasters, computers, DVD players, and other electronic devices in the 1990s because of a shortage of electricity after the Soviet Union dissolved.

The oldest university in the New World is Peru's Universidad Mayor de San Marcos, founded in 1551 by King Charles V of Spain.

Compulsory voting is enforced in nineteen countries. The penalty in these countries for not voting is usually a small fine or community service.

In Bulgaria and Greece, a nod of the head means "no."

Hawaii, Alaska, Iceland, Ireland, Crete, Malta, and New Zealand have no native land snakes.

The oldest family-owned business is the Japanese construction company Kongo Gumi, which was founded in 578 CE to build Buddhist temples and has been doing so ever since.

Most of the slaves traded by the British, Portuguese, and Spanish came from the area now comprised of Benin, Nigeria, and Togo.

South Africa has the largest percentage of people afflicted with HIV/AIDS of any country, more than 20 percent of the adult population.

Most pencils sold in Europe don't have an eraser. Most in America do. In England, erasers are called "rubbers."

The Pirahã people in Brazil don't count and have no words for numbers.

Aruba, French Guinea, Guadeloupe, Martinique, and Saint Martin are among several non-European countries in the European Union.

The rarest postage stamp in the world is the Treskilling Yellow, made in the wrong color by Sweden in 1855. There is only one known example and it is worth around $2 million.

France is by far the top tourist destination in the world. Spain and the United States follow far behind. (The United States, however, is number one in tourism earnings.)

The Feminine Mystique

VENUS AND MARS

Women are better at remembering faces than men, especially female faces.

Around 35 percent of women are super-tasters, compared with 15 percent of men, meaning they have more taste buds and perceive tastes more intensely.

Women have a better sense of smell than men.

A third of women and a fifth of men admit to being scared of spiders.

Women's favorite foods are chocolate, bread, and ice cream. Men prefer red meat, pizza, and potatoes.

Women cry five times more than men.

More men can whistle than women.

Boys get more colds than girls, but women get more than men.

Men have more car accidents than women, but drive more miles. Women have more per mile driven.

Women sleep and dream more than men.

Men snore more early in life; after menopause, women catch up.

Women are one and a half times more likely than men to be double-jointed.

Women are twice as likely as men to be able to touch their nose with their tongue.

Women fall in love more often and end relationships more often (70 percent of the time) than men.

The two highest IQ scores ever recorded belonged to women.

About 80 percent of women wash their hands after using the bathroom; only 55 percent of men do.

Even though women wash their hands more, their hands teem with a greater diversity of bacteria. Men's hands appear to be more acidic and less hospitable to germs.

In general, men can read finer print than women.

Women tend to hear better than men.

Women smile more, often out of nervousness or to be liked. Men smile more at strangers.

In a 2008 survey, more women were willing to give up sex than the Internet. The majority of men, predictably, felt otherwise.

The *American Journal of Public Health* published a study that finds fat women are 37 percent more likely to be depressed than women of average weight. The opposite was found to be true for men—skinny men were much more likely to be depressed than fat men.

Before puberty, children average about 22 percent body fat. At age eighteen, girls average 28 percent, boys average 13 percent.

Women are considered obese at 30 percent body fat, men at 25 percent.

Women lack an enzyme in the stomach that breaks down alcohol, so it goes straight into their bloodstream. Men start breaking it down right away, so drink for drink, women get tipsier.

Before the mid-1990s, gender specific testing of drugs was unknown and many drugs made for women were tested on men. This is because drug companies feared that a woman might be pregnant at the time, or become pregnant after the tests.

Women's stomachs empty slower than men's, their

hearts beat faster, and they have a higher fat content, all of which cause some drugs to react differently in women than in men.

Women come out of anesthesia faster and have more side effects from antibiotics, anti-depressants, anti-histamines, and steroids than men. Some painkillers work for women but not for men.

BREAKING THE GLASS CEILING

The first college for women in the United States was Mount Holyoke College, in Massachusetts, founded in 1837.

Elizabeth Blackwell was the first American woman to receive a medical degree, in 1849.

The first African American woman to obtain a college degree was Mary Jane Patterson at Oberlin, in 1862.

The first full-length novel, *The Tale of Genji*, was written by a Japanese woman—Murasaki Shikibu—in the eleventh century.

The first American woman to keep her maiden name was Lucy Stone of Massachusetts, a nineteenth-century women's rights activist.

In 1972, Sally Jean Priesand became the first ordained female rabbi in the United States.

PRE-HILLARY

Jeanette Rankin of Montana was the first woman elected to Congress, in 1916.

Shirley Chisholm, in 1968, was the first African American woman elected to Congress.

Nellie Tayloe Ross became the first female governor of a state in 1925. She is still the only woman governor that Wyoming has ever had.

Republican Margaret Chase Smith was the first woman to run for president of the United States and have her name placed in nomination at the convention, in 1964.

SUFFRAGETTE CITY

New Jersey allowed women to vote until politicians thought better of the idea in 1807.

> The Wyoming territory was the first portion of America to grant women the right to vote, in 1869. This proved to be a stumbling block when the territory later requested statehood and Congress tried to force them to repeal that right.

Liechtenstein didn't allow women the right to vote until 1984. Switzerland didn't allow women to vote until 1971.

HEROINES

Mary Edwards Walker was an army surgeon during the Civil War and the only woman ever awarded the Medal of Honor, in 1865. Congress revoked her medal in 1917 because she was not involved in direct combat with the enemy. Jimmy Carter restored her medal in 1977.

Annie G. Fox became the first woman to receive a Purple Heart, for being wounded during the Japanese attack on Pearl Harbor.

Helen Keller was not born deaf and blind, but a case of scarlet fever or meningitis, when she was nineteen months old, left her so.

There are more statues of Sacagawea in America than of any other woman.

BAKING WITH JULIA

Julia Child worked for the OSS during World War II and was involved in developing a repellent to keep sharks from detonating explosives targeting German submarines.

In 1958, Julia Child became the first woman to obtain the designation of full-fledged "chef."

A BUN IN THE OVEN

Nearly 25 percent of women giving birth in hospitals in America and Europe from the 1600s through the 1800s died from puerperal fever spread by the filthy hands and breath of doctors and nurses.

Pregnant women are thought to crave pickles for the salt content, since their body's salt needs greatly increase at this time.

Pregnant women can smell up to two thousand times better than when not pregnant. This may explain why pregos get morning sickness.

Worldwide, pregnancy is the number one cause of death for girls aged fifteen to nineteen.

Women who are obese have a harder time conceiving.

Scientists say that newborns look more like their fathers. Evolutionarily speaking, this helps reassure men that the baby is theirs.

C-SECTION

The Caesarean section may have been named for Caesar, but he surely wasn't delivered that way. C-sections were fatal to women at that time, and his mother was alive well into his adult life.

The first successful C-section was performed by a German pig gelder, on his wife, in 1500.

Up until the time of the Civil War, the mortality rate for women having C-sections was as high as 85 percent.

MOTHER'S MILK

Women who breast-feed have reduced risk of breast cancer over those who do not.

Roman women were happy if their husband impregnated them and a slave girl at the same time, so that they would have a built-in wet nurse.

The Roman legions often captured lactating women for sale in the slave market. The more the women lactated, the higher the price they fetched.

KEEPING ABREAST

One in two hundred women has a supernumerary (extra) nipple.

Saint Agatha is the patron saint of wet nurses, rape victims, breast diseases, and preventing volcanic eruptions. She was tortured and had her breasts cut off in the first half of the third century. Her representation is breasts on a dish and her feast day is February 5, if you wish to observe.

Foremilk is the milk first drawn from a full breast by a feeding infant. It is low in fat content, thin, and watery, which satisfies the baby's thirst. Hindmilk follows the foremilk. It is richer in fat and higher in calories, nourishing the little one.

Most mammals, including humans, exude a unique scent

THE FEMININE MYSTIQUE 107

around the mammary glands so their young can find the nipple.

Donkey milk is the animal milk closest to a human's.

A study at the University of Vienna found that large breasts are 24 percent less sensitive than smaller ones, possibly because the additional fat stretches the nerve that transmits sensation from the nipple.

SEX SYMBOLS

The female symbol (♀) represents a woman holding a mirror and is the astronomical symbol for Venus, the Roman goddess of beauty and love. The male symbol (♂) represents a shield and spear and is associated with Mars, the Roman god of war. The male and female symbols were first used by botanist Carl Linnaeus to denote the gender of plants.

CAN YOU SHOW ME WHERE IT HURTS?

In Victorian England, a woman needed a chaperone to visit the doctor. She would show the doctor on a doll where the problem was and if he needed to physically examine her, he would do so in the dark, with her under a sheet.

YOU'VE COME A LONG WAY, BABY

Marlboro cigarettes were once promoted as a woman's smoke. In 1924, they were marketed with the slogan

"Mild as May." Print ads queried, "Does smoking have any more to do with a woman's morals than the color of her hair?" Later, ads appeared telling mothers what a wonderful smoke Marlboro was.

In the 1930s, Marlboro's ivory tip was changed to red so that unsightly lipstick smears would not blemish the end of the cigarette.

In 1968, Virginia Slims were introduced with the slogan "You've come a long way, baby." This ad campaign was responsible for hooking thousands of teen girls on cigarettes.

IN VOGUE

WHAT PRICE BEAUTY?

Nightingale feces are used in facials in Hawaiian spas because the urea in the urine/poop droppings softens the skin.

Human placentas obtained from Russian maternity wards are used for facials in Beverly Hills skin care spas.

Some women have labioplasty operations to change the external appearance of the vagina.

Other women have collagen injected into the vaginal wall to narrow the vagina and enhance sexual pleasure.

Liposuction is the most common type of cosmetic surgery, followed by breast augmentation.

WHO DO YOU WANT TO LOOK LIKE?

Each year, Beverly Hills plastic surgeons compare notes to determine which star's features are the most in demand. The 2009 survey found the following stars' features were the most desired by women:

Eyes—Penélope Cruz

Nose—Katherine Heigl

Hair—Isla Fisher

Lips—Angelina Jolie

Skin—Cate Blanchett

Cheeks—Cameron Diaz

Jawline—Tyra Banks

Body—Jennifer Aniston (remember that nude *GQ* cover?). Gisele Bündchen came in second.

PALE FACES

In thirteenth-century Europe, women plucked the hairs from their heads, eyebrows, and lashes. They whitened their face and bosom with ceruse, a vinegar–powdered egg mixture that ate away at the skin and could be fatal.

Other women of the time would apply leeches to the skin or cut veins to drain blood to give them that alluring pale look.

In the 1700s, women would shave off their eyebrows and glue on mouse fur.

Queen Victoria (queen of the prudes) declared that makeup was offensive and was only worn by actors and prostitutes. Pale skin and natural complexions were the fashion for the next hundred years.

Victorian women ate arsenic to obtain a nice ashen skin tone.

Tans on women were not considered fashionable, until designer Coco Chanel was seen sporting one in Paris after a cruise on the Duke of Westminster's yacht in 1923.

ILLICIT LIPSTICK

The English Parliament banned the wearing of lipstick in 1770, stating that "women found guilty of seducing men into matrimony by cosmetic means should be tried for witchcraft."

In 1924, the New York Board of Health tried to ban the wearing of lipstick, claiming that it could poison unsuspecting men. (What about the women?)

By World War II, the pendulum had swung the other way. It was considered patriotic and a gal's duty to "put on her face."

The first "kiss-proof" lipstick hit the stores in 1950.

As of late 2007, many major brands of lipstick still contained lead.

PUTTING ON YOUR FACE

Roughly 53 percent of women will not leave home without makeup.

The most popular beauty aid for women is mascara, followed by blush, lipstick, and eye shadow.

About 28 percent of women open their mouths while applying mascara.

Some 75 percent of women will admit to applying makeup while driving.

LOVE YOUR NAILS

Nail polish was first worn five thousand years ago, in China, and served to differentiate the classes. Royalty wore bright red and black.

Nail polish came to the United States in 1907. Many women didn't know how to use it and the women's magazines of the time ran pieces on how to apply it.

THANKS *HARPER'S*

Women didn't start shaving their armpits until after a 1915 *Harper's Bazaar* cover featuring a beautiful model wearing a low-backed dress, with her skirt above her knees, no corset, and most shockingly—smooth underarms! The Wilkinson Sword Blade Company began advertising that female underarm hair was unfeminine and unhealthy shortly thereafter.

PEARLY WHITES?

Chinese people of the fifth century fancied black teeth and colored them with a dye made from eggplant skin.

Queen Elizabeth I had black teeth, due to her fondness for sugar and her poor oral hygiene. This inspired others to blacken their teeth to emulate the queen.

WHO WEARS THE PANTS?

The U.S. attorney general officially made the wearing of trousers by women legal in 1923.

In 1929, San Francisco police arrested a woman for wearing men's clothing.

Pants on women became widely acceptable in the 1950s, but the zippers were on the side. A zipper in the front would have been considered vulgar.

German fashion designer Sonja de Lennart is credited with creating the first pair of skin-tight, calf-length pants known as capris, in 1948. Designer Emilio Pucci helped to popularize them at his haute couture house on the Isle of Capri.

The early 1960s craze for capris was spurred on by Mary Tyler Moore, who stipulated in her contract that she would wear capris in one scene per episode of *The Dick Van Dyke Show*.

Levi-Strauss started selling bell-bottomed jeans in 1969.

Pantsuits began to appear in 1969, but most companies had strict rules prohibiting women from wearing them to work.

Hillary Clinton's pantsuits are designed by Susanna Chung Forest and retail for $6,350 a pop.

WHERE'D YOU GET THOSE SHOES?

Diminutive Catherine de Medici, of sixteenth-century French court fame, is credited with having the first pair of high heels, designed to make her taller.

A woman's buttocks protrude 25 percent more when wearing high heels.

The number one article of women's clothing that men have a fetish for is the high heel.

The Birkenstock family has been making footwear since at least 1744.

The U.S. Rubber Company introduced Keds in 1916.

Chuck Taylor was a high school basketball player who went to work for Converse in 1921. He suggested some improvements to the All-Star canvas basketball shoe and his name and signature were added. All-Stars are the bestselling basketball shoe of all time.

Nike shoes were born in 1972.

According to the American Academy of Orthopedic Surgeons, nine out of ten women wear shoes that are too tight.

Women's feet have been getting bigger lately. Since the mid-1980s, two and a half times more women are buying shoes size 9 and above.

BOOBY TRAPS

During the fourteenth century, very deep cleavage was the fashion. Some dresses were cut so low as to allow the nipples to be exposed.

Nipple piercing was big in the fourteenth century, because of the low-cut dresses. Curiously, there also was a brief nipple piercing craze during the Victorian era. Fashionable ladies of the time thought that nipple rings would increase the size of the breasts and are said to have enjoyed the stimulating sensation of wearing them beneath their clothes.

It took until 1935 for bra makers to figure out that women had different size breasts and start selling bras with cup sizes. British bra makers didn't catch on until the 1950s.

Imelda Marcos left behind five hundred black bras when

she and her husband fled the Philippines. One of them was bulletproof!

Howard Hughes designed a special cantilever bra for his lover Jane Russell to wear in her movies. (Jane Russell Peaks, in Alaska, are named for her ample bosom.)

Women never actually burned their bras in the 1960s. At a protest against the 1968 Miss America pageant in Atlantic City, New Jersey, several women threw bras, high heels, false eyelashes, and *Playboy* magazines into a pile, but were not able to burn them because they lacked a permit to do so.

The sports bra was invented in 1977, when Hinda Miller and Lisa Lindahl cut up a couple of jockstraps and sewed them together to create the "Jogbra."

The word "underwear" didn't enter the lexicon until the 1870s.

SHINING, GLEAMING, STREAMING . . .

The word "shampoo" comes from the Hindu word *champo*, meaning "to massage."

Modern hair conditioners were introduced at the turn of the last century to soften *men's* hair, beards, and mustaches.

In 2007, some Chinese hair salons got into a bit of trouble for recycling used condoms into hair ties.

> Around fifteen hundred Hindu women have their heads shaved each day at the Tirupati Temple in India. They see this as a sacred act. The hair is sold to make wigs for the Western market.

Wigs became fashionable in Europe in 1624, when French monarch Louis XIII began wearing one to hide his balding head. In time, the nobility's wigs got bigger and bigger, sometimes even requiring scaffolding to keep them up. Since only the rich could afford such an extravagance, the wealthy became known as "big wigs."

MAKEUP MAVENS

Avon started out as the California Perfume Company in 1886, but the name was soon changed to honor the birthplace of Shakespeare, whom the founder—David McConnell—greatly admired.

> A woman named Mabel Williams created Maybelline mascara out of black pigment and petroleum jelly. Her brother first sold it in his mail order catalog. Today, Maybelline's Great Lash is the bestselling mascara.

Max Factor was known as Max Faktorowicz before he came through Ellis Island in 1904.

Elizabeth Arden was born Florence Nightingale Graham.

The late fashion guru Mr. Blackwell was born Richard Sylvan Selzer.

Liliane Bettencourt, heir to the L'Oreal fortune, is the richest woman in the world, with an estimated wealth of about $23 billion.

BEAUTY IS IN THE EYE OF THE BEHOLDER

The Mayans found crossed eyes beautiful.

The Tiv of West Africa love big calves.

The Masai really go for black tongues and gums.

The Yapese of Micronesia admire black teeth.

Syrians dig a monobrow.

The Nilotes of East Africa knock out the front lower teeth to achieve the perfect smile.

FASHION NO-NOS

In 1574, Queen Elizabeth decreed that only royalty were allowed to wear purple silk.

In 1784, it was illegal to wear orange clothes in Holland.

In 1919, Ethelda Bleibtrey, who won three gold medals for swimming in the 1920 Olympics, was arrested for "nude swimming," when she removed her stockings at a public pool.

In 1960, the Vatican repealed the rule requiring women to wear head coverings in Catholic churches.

FASHION FIRSTS

Queen Juana of Portugal is credited with making the hoop skirt fashionable when she started wearing one in 1470 to hide a pregnancy.

The folding umbrella debuted in France in 1715.

Earmuffs were patented in 1887, the zipper in 1896.

Nylon was patented by DuPont chemist Wallace Carothers in 1937. Nylon stockings went on sale in 1940.

Velcro became available in 1978.

CLOTHES HORSE

Russian Tsarina Elizabeth, who ruled from 1741 to 1762, never wore a dress twice and left fifteen thousand in her wardrobe when she died.

BARELY THERE

The bikini debuted in 1946 at a Paris fashion show. It was named after the Bikini Atoll, an American atomic bomb test site, and was said to have created a bigger stir than the bomb itself.

A London company called Skini now makes bikinis from salmon skin.

Florida outlawed the thong bathing suit in 1990.

By 2003, thongs made up one-quarter of the $2.6 billion panty market.

Men say the thong is the sexiest article of lingerie. Women think it's the bra.

THIN IS IN

Fat was fashionable right up till the turn of the twentieth century. The biggest sex symbol of the late 1800s was two-hundred-pound Lillian Russell.

Thin girls used to write to *Ladies' Home Journal* for advice on how to *gain* weight.

The first diet pill was marketed in 1893.

Bathroom scales became popular in 1918.

The first bestselling American diet book was Lulu Ann

Peters's 1918 *Diet and Health, with Key to the Calories.*
Calories were a new concept in dieting at the time.

> A calorie is the amount of energy (heat) required to
> raise the temperature of one gram of water one de-
> gree Celsius.

The same man—S. Daniel Abraham—invented Dex-
atrim and Slim-Fast.

> Jean Nidetch founded Weight Watchers in 1961 and
> lost seventy-two pounds in a year.

The first Weight Watchers meetings were held above
a pizzeria. The owner couldn't figure out why none of
the hundreds of people lining up outside ever bought
anything.

BLACK AND BLUE

During World War II, women drew black lines up the
back of their legs with an eyebrow pencil to give the il-
lusion that they were wearing stockings (with seams),
which were unavailable at the time.

> Women in ancient Egypt thought varicose veins on
> the legs and bosom were beautiful and even colored
> them with dye.

IMMORAL BUTTONS

Buttons have been around since ancient times as decorative items. It wasn't until the thirteenth century, in Germany, that they began to be used as fasteners.

Brigham Young thought buttons were immoral.

ATTENTION SHOPPERS

The first fully enclosed shopping mall opened in Edina, Minnesota, in 1956.

Harrods in London and Macy's in Herald Square, New York, are the largest department stores in the world.

Abercrombie & Fitch first opened its doors in 1892, as an outdoors and sporting goods outfitter.

TWO OF A KLEIN

Clothing designer Anne Klein's real name was Hannah Golofski.

Donna Karan took over the Anne Klein line after Klein's death in 1974. In 1989, she left to start DKNY.

In 2004, the Calvin Klein Company told all employees that they must adhere to the "Calvin Klein aesthetic" in the office. No photos, toys, mementos, awards, or flowers (except white ones) would be permitted on desks. All office supplies on desks had to be black or white. Even the ink in the pens had to be black. Acceptable screensavers had to be downloaded from the company.

LOVE AND MARRIAGE

LOCKING LIPS

The scientific study of kissing is called philematology.

More than 90 percent of the world's peoples kiss. The Somalis don't, but chimps and bonobos do.

Two-thirds of people tilt their heads to the right when kissing.

One study indicates that people who kiss their spouse good-bye in the morning tend to make more money.

The longest kiss in film history lasted three and a half minutes. It was between Jane Wyman and Ray Tooney in the 1941 movie *You're in the Army Now*.

In sixteenth-century Naples, public kissing carried the death penalty.

There is a twelve-dollar fine for public kissing in Delhi, India. A warrant for Richard Gere's arrest was issued after he jokingly kissed an Indian actress in public in 2007.

England's King Henry VI outlawed kissing to prevent the spread of disease.

CHILD BRIDES

Roughly 74 percent of the brides in the Democratic Republic of the Congo are teens.

Girls can get married at age eight in Saudi Arabia.

In Nepal, 7 percent of the girls are married before age ten.

In five South American countries, the legal age for girls to marry is twelve.

In Chad and Gambia, 100 percent of the men are married by age fifty.

DIVORCE COURT

Guatemala has the lowest divorce rate of any country, the Maldives the highest.

Divorces are not permitted in Malta or the Philippines.

People who marry in their early twenties are most likely to get divorced.

LOVE AND MARRIAGE 125

Nevada has the highest percentage of divorces of any U.S. state; New Jersey the lowest.

Common-law marriages can be contracted in eleven states. There is no such thing as a common-law divorce.

In some Muslim countries, a Sunni man can divorce his wife simply by saying "*talaq*" ("I divorce you") three times.

MULTIPLE PARTNERS

One Giovanni Vigliotto married 104 women between 1941 and 1981. He was sentenced to twenty-eight years in jail for bigamy in 1983.

In 1922, twenty-four-year-old Englishwoman Theresa Vaughn, was convicted of marrying sixty-two men in five years.

Brigham Young had fifty-five wives.

IT'S GOOD TO BE KING!

The king of Swaziland has his first two wives picked for him by the national councilors. They do not officially become his wives until they become pregnant by him. The king is expected to take many wives. He often selects one during the annual Reed Dance, where up to fifty thousand young maidens in traditional garb, wielding machetes, parade topless past him. The current king has thirteen wives. His father had seventy, and more than one thousand grandchildren.

CHEATIN' HEARTS

Ashley Madison is a matchmaker website for married people who want to cheat. It currently has 2.6 million members.

S-Check is a spray that is used to check someone's underwear for the presence of seminal fluid.

BY THE POWER VESTED IN ME

The Catholic Church did not require a priest to be at weddings until 1563.

Ship's captains have no special rights to marry people.

Officers of the Salvation Army can only marry other officers of the Army.

WHO FUNDS THESE STUDIES?

Research suggests older men can reduce their risk of prostate cancer through regular masturbation. It seems regular servicing helps flush out cancer-causing chemicals. Curiously, self-gratification has the opposite effect on younger men.

In studies, men find a woman much more sexually attractive when she is dressed in red, and will spend more money on a date with her. Red does not, however, affect a man's perceptions about her likeability, intelligence, or kindness.

MEMBERS ONLY

In 1640, condoms were made of dried pig's intestines. They had to be soaked in milk to soften them before using.

Early rubber condoms were very thick and made to be washed out and reused.

The word "condom" is from the Latin *condon*, meaning "receptacle," not from the apocryphal "Dr. Condom or Condon."

In Stockholm, those in need can call a "condom ambulance," a white truck, adorned with a red winged condom on the side, that will deliver to the door a condom ten-pack.

During the 1200s, European noblemen openly displayed their genitals through a hole in the crotch of their tights.

Semen travels at 28 miles per hour when ejaculated.

Men produce fifty thousand sperm per minute.

In the past twenty-five years, about 65 percent of newborn American boys were circumcised.

Only about 15 percent of the world's males are circumcised. It is rarely practiced in Europe, Latin and South America, or most of Asia.

There is a penis museum in Iceland.

The Kama Sutra classified men by the size of their penis—hare, bull, or horse. Women were ranked by the size of their vagina—deer, mare, or elephant. The greatest sexual satisfaction was to be found with a mate of similar size.

VICTORIA'S SECRETS

In August 1971, *Penthouse* was the first major men's magazine to publish full frontal nudity. In January 1972, *Playboy* followed suit.

Scientific research has demonstrated that the combined smell of Good & Plenty and cucumber increases the blood flow to a woman's genitals, as does the aroma of baby powder. The aroma of pumpkin and lavender has the same effect on men.

The smell of cherries, barbecue, and men's cologne turns women off.

The clitoris is an organ that has no purpose other than sexual stimulation.

There is no biological need for a woman to have an orgasm. The only female animal known to do so is the human.

Women who have circumcised partners are less likely to get cervical cancer.

Vibrators were sold in the Sears catalog in 1918 as an item "every woman appreciates."

Affluent Roman ladies could keep *spadones*, or castrated sex slaves.

Ancient Egyptian women used crocodile dung as a contraceptive (you know where they put it). Roman women preferred pepper.

During the Great Depression, American women would douche with Lysol after sex. *(Do not try this!)*

LOVE STINKS

Women who ovulate prefer the scent of, and are sexually attracted to, men who have immune-system genes that differ from their own. Taking the Pill shifts a woman's preferences toward men that have similar genes, so that when she goes off the Pill, her attraction for her mate may go off too. It's best to pick a partner before going on the Pill.

TOO MUCH OF A GOOD THING

Persistent sexual arousal syndrome, also known as *iku iku byo* ("come come disease") in Japan, is an affliction of a small percentage of women in which they experience constant sexual stimulation and may have as many as three hundred orgasms throughout the day, whether they are aroused or not. It is most common in postmenopausal women who have had hormone treatment.

"G" MARKS THE SPOT

In 2008, the mythically elusive female G-spot was captured on ultrasound for the first time. The thing is, only about 25 percent of the women scanned seemed to have one. The University of L'Aquila (Italy) study found that none of the women without G-spots ever had vaginal orgasms, while most of the G-spot ladies did. Apparently, the G-spot women have a thicker area of tissue between the urethra and vagina, on the front vaginal wall, that responds to stimulation from penetration.

AROUND THE WORLD (IN BED)

The Hottentot people of Africa have a condition called "steatopygia," which gives them copious amounts of fat on their buttocks.

Hottentot men think twins are evil and come from having two testicles, so of course, they cut one off. Likewise, the Ponapeans of Micronesia remove one of a boy's testicles at puberty.

The Siriono people of Bolivia remove ticks and lice from one another and eat them before sex, as a kind of foreplay.

On ceremonial occasions, central Australian Walibri men from different tribes greet each other by shaking penises, not hands.

Women give the gifts on Valentine's Day in Japan. It's the men's turn on March 15, known as White Day, when the traditional gift is white chocolate and marshmallows, or anything in a white box.

THE DAYS OF YORE

During Shakespeare's time, young maidens would put a peeled apple under their arms and then give it to their beaus to eat.

Saint Jerome forbade the nuns under his charge from eating beans because they resemble testicles, not to mention that farting "tickled the genitals."

A feudal lord was entitled to deflower girls living on his lands on their wedding night, under a rule referred to as "right of the first night."

NO GIRLS ALLOWED

Menstruating women are forbidden to enter Hindu temples in Bali.

Menstruating Muslim women cannot enter a mosque, touch a Koran, or even pray at home.

Mount Athos, in Macedonia, is a self-governed monastic state comprised of twenty monasteries. The monks ban all females, human or animal. However, chickens, which lay eggs, and female cats, which help control the rat population, are tolerated.

BIG BROTHER

Before 1962, sodomy was a felony in all fifty states. Illinois was the first state to legalize it. Sodomy was still a crime in many states up until the Supreme Court ruled against such laws in 2003.

THE OLDEST PROFESSION

Theodora, sixth-century empress of the Byzantine Empire and Orthodox Church saint, was a prostitute.

> Japanese prostitutes of the seventeenth century were kept in special walled districts and only allowed out once a year, to see the cherry blossoms and visit dying relatives.

The first female geisha appeared in 1751; before this, they were all males.

> St. Louis legalized prostitution in 1870.

Prostitution is currently legal in Rhode Island, as long as it takes place in a private residence.

> The famous Texas whorehouse, the Chicken Ranch, got its name during the Depression. Business was so slow, they began accepting chickens for payment and the place was soon overrun with them.

X'S AND O'S

Ladies' Home Journal lost 75,000 subscribers in 1906, when they ran a series of articles on venereal disease.

Cupid was a symbol of pedophile love in ancient Greece.

At one time, women used half a lemon or an orange peel as a diaphragm.

The first human artificial insemination was performed in 1785.

The median number of opposite-sex partners adult men claim to have had is six or seven. Women claim four.

In Egyptian mythology, the god Saa (also spelled Sia) was responsible for protecting the genitals of the dead. (Talk about a specific deity.)

A 2008 study at New Mexico State University in Las Cruces found that self-absorbed, devious, thrill-seeking men do better with the ladies.

BLINDED BY SCIENCE

IT'S ELEMENTARY

The most common elements in Earth's crust are oxygen, silicon, and iron, in that order.

The most common elements in the universe are hydrogen and helium.

The most expensive metal is rhodium, which sells for more than $176,000 per kilogram. Platinum and gold, numbers two and three, trail far behind.

The metal lithium, the lightest solid element, is half as heavy as water. It is so soft it can be cut with a butter knife.

One cubic foot of osmium, the heaviest element, weighs 1,140 pounds.

Helium will remain liquid right down to absolute zero.

Nitrous oxide is called "laughing gas" because it makes you feel happy. In the early 1800s, laughing gas parties were popular. It was at one such party, in 1844, that a dentist first realized the potential use for the gas as a painkiller.

Emeralds and aquamarines are the same mineral. Emeralds just have a little more chromium, which makes them green.

Silver is the best naturally occurring conductor of heat and electricity.

Fluorine reacts with almost every other element to form extremely tight bonds, resulting in some of the most inert compounds known, such as Teflon.

Tungsten does not melt until it reaches a temperature of 6,192°F.

Plutonium is the most dangerous element.

The half-life of bismuth-214 is 19.7 minutes; plutonium-239, 24,110 years; and uranium-238, 4.46 billion years.

In 1951, there actually was a "Gilbert U-238 Atomic Energy Lab" toy on the market that exposed kids to radioactive uranium-bearing rocks containing isotope U-238, which is now linked to leukemia, lymphoma, other cancers, and Gulf War Syndrome.

ALL THAT GLITTERS

The Aztec word for gold is *teocuitlatl*, meaning "excrement of the gods."

In all of history, *only* 161,000 tons of gold have been mined, enough to fill two Olympic-size swimming pools.

In 1999, the NEAR spacecraft detected more gold on the asteroid Eros than has ever been mined on Earth.

Gold is virtually indestructable. About 85 percent of all the gold ever mined is still being used.

A liquid suspension of gold is a good anti-inflammatory and was once used to treat rheumatoid arthitis.

The United States has the most gold bullion, but if you include decorative gold, India has the most gold.

Some 70 percent of the world's gold goes into jewelry.

HIGH TALKING

Helium makes your voice high-pitched because it is less dense than air, making the sound waves travel faster. When these fast-moving waves hit the air outside your mouth, they slow down and get closer together, raising the high frequency (pitch). If you and the listener were both in a room filled with helium, your voice would sound normal, as there would be no change in frequency.

If you were to breathe in a gas that was denser than air, your voice would become much deeper, almost demonic. (These gases are very poisonous, so don't get any ideas.)

A POT TO YOU-KNOW-WHAT IN

Phosphorus was discovered in 1675, when a German alchemist tried to create gold from urine by storing pots of pee in his basement for months on end. The resultant glowing, waxy goo spontaneously burst into flames. Until an industrial means was invented to manufacture phosphorus, soldiers supplied endless buckets of the raw material.

In the Middle Ages, urine was used to make saltpeter for gunpowder.

Natural gas is mostly methane and has no odor. For safety reasons, trace amounts of t-butyl mercaptan are added to give it that funky rotten cabbage smell. The human nose can detect one part of natural gas odorant in 50 million.

LIVING PLANET

Life can flourish at great temperature extremes, such as above 230°F around thermal vents and below 5°F in permafrost.

There are probably about 14 million different species on Earth.

Only about 15 percent of the species in the world are believed to have been discovered so far.

Of the world's known species, 99 percent are smaller than a bumblebee.

DOUBLE HELIX

An unwound strand of DNA would stretch more than six and a half feet.

The grayfish has the most chromosomes of all creatures—two hundred.

DNA studies have determined that all humans alive today are related to one female nicknamed "African Eve," who lived in northeastern Africa about 140,000 years ago.

The world has six distinct genetic population groups that correspond to the following geographic areas: Africa, the Americas, East Asia, Eurasia, Oceania, and the Kalash, a small ethnic group of about six thousand people that lives in the Hindu Kush of northwest Pakistan.

About ten thousand years ago, the first person with blue eyes was born somewhere in northern Europe after a single genetic mutation. All blue-eyed people today can thank this one individual.

UNSEEN WORLD?

Thiomargarita namibiensis, or sulfur pearl, is the largest known bacteria, reaching a width of 0.75 millimeters (0.029 inches), making it easily visble to the naked eye.

There are so many bacteria and archaea (single-celled organisms) in the world that if you lined them up end to end, they would reach to the end of the visible universe, or 10 billion light-years.

There are ten times as many bacteria in the human body as human cells.

Some bacteria can live two miles underground on the energy given off by radioactive decay.

Eight-million-year-old bacteria have been revived from Antarctic ice.

MAY CAUSE SIDE EFFECTS

Viagra was first tested as a drug for treating angina in a Welsh mining town in 1992. The drug—sildenafil citrate—didn't do much for the male patients' angina, but they sure began paying a lot of attention to their nurses.

The cholesterol pill Lipitor is far and away the best-selling drug in the world, followed by the blood thinner Plavix and the heartburn drug Nexium.

Antidepressants are the number one prescribed class of drug in the United States, followed by hypertension medications.

It takes, on average, ten years for a new drug to make it from the lab to the market.

One of Kaopectate's main ingredients used to be clay.

TO INFINITY AND BEYOND

Space shuttle astronauts can pick from a menu of one hundred foods and fifty beverages to bring on their mission.

Chinese astronauts may be eating silkworms on future, long-distance space flights.

Astronauts drink recycled urine, sweat, exhaled water vapor, and bathing water.

Astronauts can sleep free-floating or zipped into a sleeping bag. They also can strap a pillow to their heads if desired.

THE RIGHT STUFF

Gus Grissom almost became the first person to die on a space mission, in 1961, when his Liberty Bell 7 capsule sank after splashdown in the Pacific. Sadly, he did die six years later, along with fellow astronauts Roger Chafee and Ed White, when the *Apollo 1* command module caught fire in a launch simulation test.

The only people to die *in* outer space were the three cosmonauts on board *Soyuz 11*, who suffocated in 1971 because of a faulty air valve.

All three fatal NASA disasters occurred in the same calendar week—the three *Apollo 1* astronauts died in a fire on January 27, 1967; the shuttle *Challenger* blew up on January 28, 1986; and the shuttle *Columbia* disintegrated on February 1, 2003.

The only survivors of the *Columbia* disaster were a bunch of nematodes (tiny worms) that were on board for biological tests.

WOOOSH!

At liftoff, the shuttle's solid rocket boosters consume eleven thousand pounds of fuel a second.

The shuttle is white and black and the boosters orange because these are the colors of the materials from which they are made. They are not painted, so as to reduce weight.

BILLIONS AND BILLIONS

There are about five thousand stars visible to the naked eye in the Northern Hemisphere under ideal conditions.

The nearest star to the Sun is Proxima Centauri at 4.22 light-years, or 24.8 trillion miles, away.

In the Milky Way, the farthest star from Earth is about 160,000 light-years away, farther than the closest galaxy.

The closest galaxy to the Milky Way is the dwarf elliptical galaxy Sagittarius, discovered in 1994. It is fifty thousand light-years from the edge of the Milky Way and eighty thousand light-years from Earth.

On the other extreme, the most distant known galaxy from Earth is about 15 billion light-years away.

The most distant object that can be seen with the naked eye in the night sky is the Andromeda galaxy, about 2.5 million light-years from Earth.

EARTHWISE

Earth hurtles through space at a speed of 18.5 miles per second.

The morning moon is in front of Earth as it orbits the Sun. Face it and you are looking in the direction Earth is moving.

Every 800,000 years or so, Earth's magnetic poles flip—the north pole becomes the south pole, and vice versa. Scientists think this may happen again in another 1,500 years.

The oldest minerals on Earth are Australian zircons formed 4.3 billion years ago.

🌰 THIS IS THE END

Scientists have calculated that the odds of Earth being destroyed or civilization ending in the following ways are:

Asteroid impact—1 in 700,000

Supernova—1 in 10,000,000

Gamma ray burst—1 in 14,000,000

Black hole—1 in 1,000,000,000,000

🌰 ALL WET

There is the same quantity of water on Earth today as there was 4 billion years ago.

Only 1 percent of the world's water is fresh and unfrozen.

The tallest wave ever recorded was one of 1,740 feet in Lituya Bay, Alaska. A landslide launched into the bay by an earthquake in 1958 caused it.

THESE OLD BONES

The oldest fossils ever found are those of 3.5-billion-year-old bacteria in northwest Australia.

The oldest known vertebrate is a jawless fish that lived in China 500 million years ago.

The longest dinosaur tail was forty-three feet long and belonged to *Diplodocus*, a giant herbivore that roamed North America 145 million years ago.

The largest dinosaur coprolite (poop, that is) was found in Saskatchewan. It is eighteen inches long and is believed to have been deposited by a *T. rex*.

The biggest primate in the fossil record is the aptly named *Gigantopithecus*. This guy lived in present-day China and Southeast Asia, from about 13 million to fifty thousand years ago. It stood ten feet tall on its hind legs and weighed about six hundred pounds.

STORM STORIES

The most severe tornado classification on the Fujita scale is an F6, with winds of 319 to 379 miles per hour. So far, one has never been recorded.

A swarm of more than sixty tornadoes occurred on February 19, 1884, which may have killed as many as eight hundred people in eight Southeastern states. A swarm of 148 tornadoes killed 303 people in eleven Midwestern states on April 3, 1974.

There have been many documented accounts of it "raining" fish and frogs, after they were presumably sucked up from the surface of a body of water by a tornado or strong storm and dropped some distance away.

Lightning does not always produce thunder.

Rocket launches, nuclear explosions, and volcanic eruptions can all trigger lightning.

🔰 KATRINA AND THE WAVES

The World Meteorological Association started giving hurricanes women's names in 1953 (much to the chagrin of feminists). In 1979, the association began alternating women's names with men's names.

No hurricane names start with Q, U, X, Y, or Z.

Famous storms, like Katrina in 2005, have their names retired.

Ivan generated estimated 132-foot waves in the Gulf of Mexico in 2004.

In 1943, U.S. Air Force Colonel Joseph B. Duckworth became the first pilot to fly a plane into a hurricane, after some British pilots bet him that his AT-6 Texan training plane couldn't do it. He won the bet.

NO TWO ARE ALIKE

Things like pollution, pollen, soot, and dust can cause the occasional red, yellow, or black snowfall.

There is something called "watermelon snow" that is reddish and tastes like watermelon because of a red alga that can grow in snowdrifts. It may taste good, but it will cause diarrhea.

Different shaped snowflakes form at different temperatures. Hexagonal crystals form just below freezing. Crystals become columnar at lower temperatures and then become hexagonal again at really cold temperatures.

The snowiest city in the continental United States is Marquette, Michigan, with a mean annual snowfall of 130.6 inches.

In a twenty-four-hour period from January 25 to 26, 1979, the temperature in Browning, Montana, fell one hundred degrees, from 44°F to -56°F.

Contrary to what you may see in movies, loud noises do not trigger avalanches.

The biggest verifiable hailstone is a foot-and-a-half-diameter monster that fell in Coffeyville, Kansas, in 1970.

Every so often large chunks of ice fall from the clear blue sky, some weighing as much as two hundred pounds. No one is sure why.

Each winter 1,000,000,000,000,000,000,000,000 snowflakes fall from the sky. While technically speaking no two are molecularly identical, some look pretty darn similar.

DIRTY PLANET

According to the World Health Organization, 1.6 million people die each year from indoor pollution.

Cairo has more particulate pollution than any other city.

Sixteen of the twenty most polluted cities in world are in

China. Three of the most polluted areas in the world are in Russia.

> The worst air quality (particle pollution) in all of America is in the Los Angeles–Long Beach–Riverside area in California.

New Jersey, Pennsylvania, and California, in that order, have the most toxic waste sites in the United States.

> Between December 5 and 9, 1952, a cloud of deadly smog, laced with sulfur dioxide, nitrogen oxides, and soot, hung over London, killing at least four thousand people. Known as the "Great Smog of 1952," it brought the city to a standstill.

In 1962, volunteer firefighters in Centralia, Pennsylvania, set fire to the local garbage dump in an abandoned strip mine pit. The fire burned into the coal mine tunnels beneath the town and has been burning ever since, making the town unlivable and reducing the population from one thousand in 1981 to just nine in 2007.

> A recent study in the *New England Journal of Medicine* found that decreasing levels of air pollution in the last twenty years have added five months to the average American's life span.

Livestock are responsible for the emission of more greenhouse gases than all the cars, trucks, and planes put together. One cow puts out about the same amount as driving an SUV 6,200 miles.

The "Great Pacific Garbage Patch" is a huge expanse of refuse, primarily plastics, two times the size of Texas, which is floating around in the Northern Pacific.

One acre of woodland can remove up to thirteen tons of gases and dust from the environment.

Recycling one ton of paper can save seventeen trees.

UP, UP, AND AWAY

Jet fuel is not made up of any fancy chemicals, just kerosene.

A 747 burns about one gallon of fuel for every second it is in flight. On a ten-hour flight, that may add up to 36,000 gallons. That averages out to about five gallons per mile.

An early parachute was invented in the 1470s as a way to escape a burning building.

Each year, about a dozen U.S. commercial flights have to make emergency landings because of bird strikes. Birds hit about 4,700 flights a year.

MOVING AT THE SPEED OF . . .

A beam of light moves at different speeds through different materials, causing it to bend toward the slower material when traveling between the two at an angle.

Light in a vacuum travels at 186,383 miles per second (mps); through water at 139,715 mps; through glass at 120,000 mps; and through a diamond at 76,976 mps.

IS IT COLD IN HERE?

Anders Celsius, inventor of the Celsius scale in 1741, first had 100° as the freezing point of water and 0° as the boiling point. These were reversed in 1749.

The only point where the temperature reads the same on the Celsius and Fahrenheit scales is -40°.

Scientists can come within a fraction of a degree of absolute zero (-459.7°F), the coldest possible temperature in the universe, in the lab, but quantum fluctuations in molecular motion make it impossible to reach that minimum.

The Kelvin scale is a temperature scale where absolute zero is zero, or 0 K. No degree sign is used to represent Kelvin units.

The Tokamak Fusion Test Reactor in Princeton, New Jersey, once produced the highest man-made temperature, of 510 million°C.

Seawater generally freezes at 28°F.

Air is a poor conductor of heat. Hence, most good insulating materials have lots of air spaces within.

Metal feels cold because it is a good conductor of heat, so it draws heat away from the skin.

NO STATIC AT ALL

The first regularly scheduled AM radio broadcasts began in 1916, when 8XK in Wilkinsburg, Pennsylvania, went on the air.

FM radio signals go straight out into space. AM signals bounce off the ionosphere and can travel thousands of miles around the globe.

AM radio signals are one thousand feet long compared to FM signals, which are only ten feet long. Because of this, AM signals will bend more easily around things like mountains, whereas the shorter FM signals can't, causing them to fade out.

MA BELL

AT&T and Bell Labs introduced the U.S. area code system in 1947. The first and third numbers were assigned based on the population density of the area. The more populated an area, the lower its code was. The rationale being that on rotary phones, a low number like 212 for New York City, had a shorter "dial pull," requiring less "work" to dial. Northern New Jersey, with 201, has the lowest code because that is where Bell Labs was located.

England had the first emergency call number—999.

The Universal Emergency Call System in the United States started in 1968. Most of AT&T Bell's service numbers ended in 11, and 211 through 811 were already in use, so by default, 911 was chosen.

The first working fax machine preceded the telephone, in 1861.

GOING METRIC

The metric system was created during the French Revolution.

The International Prototype Kilogram is a platinum-iridium alloy, created in 1879, that is the standard by which all the world's weight measures are calibrated. It is locked in a Paris vault and is only brought out on very rare occasions.

The length of a meter is defined by the distance light travels in a vacuum in 1/299,792,458 seconds.

The system of measurement used in America is called U.S. customary measure.

In 1975, the U.S. Congress passed the Metric Conversion Act to help begin the transition of Americans from customary measure to the metric system used by the rest of the world. It died a quiet death due to lack of interest.

NASA's Mars Climate Orbiter burned up in the Martian atmosphere because all the contractors who built it used metric measures, but Lockheed Martin used customary (American) measure for the thruster data.

DOES ANYBODY REALLY KNOW WHAT TIME IT IS?

Thank the Babylonians for having sixty seconds in a minute and sixty minutes in an hour. They believed sixty to be a mystical number (because no lower number could be divided by more numbers), so developed a base-sixty counting system.

The Babylonian love of numbers that are multiples of sixty also gives us a circle with 360 degrees. They noticed that the sun took about 360 days to complete its annual circuit through the sky and divided its circular path into 360 degrees to track each day's passage of the journey.

The degree sign (°) is thought to be an ancient representation of the sun.

The Egyptians gave us the twenty-four-hour day. They divided the night into twelve segments based on the rising of the twelve constellations; divided the daytime into ten segments for the ten positions of the sun; and left one segment each for dawn and dusk.

During the French Revolution, the country had a ten-day week, a ten-hour day, hours comprised of one hundred minutes, and each minute comprised of one hundred seconds. This system was used for twelve years, until Napoleon took power.

The seven-day week comes from Genesis—God created the world in six days and rested on the seventh.

January 1 became the first day of the year starting in 153 BCE, when the new Roman consuls took over the government on that day and decreed it the beginning of the new year.

Before the 1800s, there were no standard time zones. Each town had its own time, as adjusted to the local solar noon.

Standard time zones were introduced in 1883 to accommodate railroad schedules.

Some counties in Indiana are in the Central Time Zone, while most are in the Eastern Time Zone. They have been switching between zones for years. Before April 2005, only parts of the state observed daylight savings time.

Earth's rotation slows by three milliseconds per century, so during the time of the dinosaurs, a day was only twenty-three hours long.

To compensate for the slowing of Earth's rotation, a "leap second" is added every few years.

The length of a second used to correspond to 1/86,400 of a mean solar day.

Today, the length of a second is determined using the frequency of the radiation absorbed or emitted by an atom of cesium-133—9,192,631,770 cycles per second.

The longest recognized period of time is the *kalpa*, which is Hindu for 4.32 billion years.

GOIN' MOBILE

The first motorized vehicle was a steam-powered tractor built by Nicolas Cugnot for the French army to pull artillery pieces in 1769. It moved along at only 2.5 miles per hour and never caught on.

Karl Friedrich Benz built the first true automobile with a gasoline-powered internal combustion engine in 1885–86 in Germany.

The first electric-powered carriage was built in Scotland in the 1930s.

In the early 1900s, Ben Holt, of Stockton, California, invented the first tracked vehicle that spread the weight of the load over a large area to prevent the vehicle from getting stuck in the mud. A friend of his suggested that it looked like a caterpillar, and the rest is history.

The first person killed in a car accident was Londoner Bridget Driscoll, who in 1896 was run over by an auto traveling at the reckless speed of 4 miles per hour.

Talking on the cell phone ranks as the sixth most common cause of car accidents, just behind adjusting the radio.

ON THE ROAD AGAIN

It takes about four years for a new car design to reach the showroom.

The Mitsubishi logo—three diamonds—represents a stylized airplane propeller. The company used to make the Japanese Zero fighter planes during World War II.

The Subaru logo—six stars—represents the Pleiades star cluster in Taurus called *Subaru* in Japan. The six stars symbolize the six companies that merged in 1953 to make cars.

The first official stop sign was put up in Detroit, Michigan, in 1915.

There were a number of background colors for stop signs until the 1920s, when they were standardized to yellow. They didn't become red until 1954.

National School Bus Chrome Yellow is the standard school bus color in the United States. It was adopted in 1939 and is kept today since bus makers find it cheaper to paint them all the same color.

The roofs of school buses are white to keep them cooler inside in hot weather. It's a state law in Texas.

DOOMSDAY DEVICE

The Large Hadron Collider (LHC) near Geneva, Switzerland, is a seventeen-mile-diameter particle accelerator designed to collide protons with energies of 7 trillion electron volts apiece, moving at approximately 99.999999 percent of the speed of light.

> To get up to proper speed, the protons need to make almost 17 million revolutions in the LHC—a distance of about 279.6 million miles.

One bad solder connection on the $9 billion LHC caused a spark that blew a hole in its super-cooled helium blanket, which will cost $21 million to fix.

> Some people fear that a mini black hole created by the LHC will swallow Earth. Independent studies have concluded this is extremely unlikely.

KILOGIRLS

Before the invention of computers, humans called "calculators" did number crunching. As the calculators were by and large women, their computing power was measured in "kilogirls."

> America's first electronic computer, called ENIAC, was developed to calculate artillery firing tables for American guns in World War II. It wasn't operational until 1946, too late for the war.

"Giant Brain," as the press referred to ENIAC, was comprised of 17,468 vacuum tubes, 7,200 crystal diodes, 1,500 relays, 70,000 resistors, 10,000 capacitors, and around 5 million soldered connections. It weighed in at 30 tons and occupied 680 square feet. Early on, the tubes blew out so often that the computer was only functional half of the time.

The abacus is still used widely throughout Africa and Asia.

POWERFUL DATA

The United States gets about 19 percent of its power from 104 nuclear reactors at sixty-three plants.

Depending on the blend, gasoline can contain from 150 to 1,000 different chemical compounds.

A gallon of gas represents what was once about one hundred tons of plant matter.

The United States gets 6 percent of its electricity from hydropower production. Washington, Oregon, and California are the top producers.

More than half of the world's population relies on dung, wood, crop waste, or coal to meet their basic energy needs.

Windmills were invented in Persia in the ninth century.

IT'S ELECTRIC

When you rub a balloon against your sweater, you are creating more electrons (negative charges) on its surface. They cause the balloon to stick to a wall, which has a more positive charge, because opposites attract.

When you remove your knit hat in wintertime, electrons are added to your hair. Because all your hairs now have the same charge, they repel each other and stand up.

BRIGHT IDEA

Joseph Swan patented a carbon-filament lightbulb in England, ten months before Edison did so in America. Edison made big money from the lightbulb, upsetting Swan, who sued for patent infringement in England and won.

NUMB3RS

Ancient accountants appear to have been the first people to write things down. The oldest known recorded information is on European bones marked with what look like tallies to record numbers that date from around 30,000 BCE.

Arabic numbers were invented in India in 500 BCE.

Englishman Robert Recorde introduced the world to the equal sign (=) in 1557. He chose a pair of parallel lines because "no two things can be more equal."

Autistic savant Daniel Tammet of England once memorized pi to 22,514 digits in 5 hours and 9 minutes.

NEWER ISN'T ALWAYS BETTER

Knives made from obsidian are the sharpest possible. Properly worked, an obsidian blade's edge can approach the thickness of one molecule and is much smoother and sharper than even surgical steel.

The Haya people of Tanzania have been making high-grade steel for two thousand years.

YOU: THE CHAPTER

OF OVA AND SPERM

The largest cell in the human body is the ovum (egg), which is visible to the naked eye.

An adolescent girl has about 34,000 undeveloped eggs, of which only about 350 will mature before she reaches menopause.

The smallest cell in the human body is the sperm. It would take 175,000 sperm to equal the weight of one ovum.

CELLULAR SIGHTS

Look up at the sky on a bright day. Those little starlike things you see shooting around are white blood cells moving through the capillaries in your retinas.

There are two hundred different cell types in the human body and more than 100 trillion cells.

THE SKINNY

The keratin layer of dead skin is thickest on the hands and feet. It's this layer that absorbs moisture during a long bath. This is why only the hands and feet wrinkle when soaked for a long time.

> People with the genetic defects Naegeli syndrome or dermatopathia pigmentosa reticularis have no fingerprints.

Books used to occasionally be bound with the skin of executed prisoners.

> The human body sheds about fifty thousand dead skin cells every minute.

NO SWEAT

The only parts of the body that don't sweat are the eardrums, the margins of the lips, the nail bed, and the tip of the penis.

> Body odor comes from bacteria digesting fatty secretions of the apocrine sweat glands found on the armpits, genitals, and anus.

Breasts are really modified apocrine (sweat) glands.

WEIGHTY MATTERS

One-third of Americans are obese and another third are overweight.

The number of obese Americans has doubled since 1980.

On average, Americans got eight and a half pounds heavier from 1991 to 2000.

California is the only state where the rate of obesity is not on the rise.

Once you reach adulthood, the total number of fat cells in your body stays the same; they just get bigger or smaller.

Diet and exercise reduce the size of your fat cells. Only liposuction can reduce their number.

People who eat breakfast and dinner out a lot are more likely to be obese.

Tobacco use is the number one cause of preventable death; obesity is number two.

A person who weighs 154 pounds contains 95 pounds of oxygen.

In California, it's illegal to use human medical waste to power a vehicle. This law came to light after a plastic surgeon started using fat he liposuctioned out of his patients as biodiesel fuel for his car.

Doctors now can insert tubes with cameras up a woman's vagina to help in performing stomach-shrinking surgeries. (They can also remove gall bladders, kidneys, and appendixes transvaginally.)

THANKS, EVE

The Adam's apple is a thyroid cartilage. The male version is bigger. Females have more fat in their necks, which hides theirs.

> The name Adam's apple comes from the biblical story in Eden where Eve gave Adam the apple to eat and it got stuck in his throat, symbolizing his shame.

TURN AND COUGH

A hernia is a weakness or hole in a tissue that will allow an organ to protrude through the rupture.

> A doctor makes patients cough during a hernia exam to feel for the bulge with his finger. He makes them turn their heads so they don't cough in his face.

GERMY WORLD

A recent study on hand germs found that individuals have few types of bacteria in common with each other. Even the left hand and right hand of the same individual only share about 17 percent of the same bacterial types.

> Every flu strain has its origins in Asia. Flu viruses are constantly circulating and mutating among the countries of China, South Korea, Singapore, and the Philippines. Travelers spread them around the world.

The germiest thing in the average hospital room is the

TV remote. It harbors more germ-resistant *Staphylococcus* bacteria than even the toilet handle.

🌰 LICK YOUR WOUNDS

Licking wounds may actually be beneficial. Human saliva contains compounds that fight infection and encourage healing. This is why a cut in the mouth heals much quicker than a cut elsewhere on the body.

FUNNY BONES

The smallest bone in the human body is the stapes, or stirrup, found in the middle ear. It is only 0.07 inches long.

The only bone in the body not connected to another bone is the hyoid. It sits in the back of the throat and is supported by thyroid cartilage and is attached to the root of the tongue.

GRAY MATTER

The brain is 70 percent fat.

Men's brains process women's voices differently than men's voices (no, they don't tune them out). The female voice seems to get a male's attention. For this reason, a woman's voice (known as "Bitchin' Betty") is used in F-16 fighter jet and Apache helicopter cockpits for warnings.

Naegleria fowleri is a freshwater amoeba, commonly found in warm bodies of freshwater, that can swim up the nose and into the brain, where it will fatally destroy brain tissue.

MELLOW YELLOW

On average, people should urinate every two to four hours.

> Five million American kids suffer from nocturnal enuresis—better known as bedwetting.

OOOOH THAT SMELL

Our sense of smell is ten thousand times more sensitive than our sense of taste.

> Smell is the sense with the most direct connections to the behavior centers of the brain, so odors are subject to the least rational thought and self-control. Smells can trigger memories and actions that we are unaware of.

Feet sometimes smell like cheese because very similar bacteria cause both odors.

> The typical male fart contains around half a cup of gas, a female fart a third of a cup.

EYE SEE

In one hour of reading a book, eye muscles make ten thousand coordinated movements. (Tired yet?)

Calm people blink fifteen times a minute, nervous people fifty. Liars do more blinking than those telling the truth. Babies only blink twice a minute.

MUSCLE BOUND

The strongest muscle based on size is the masseter, which is in the jaw.

The muscle that can pull the greatest weight is the soleus, which is located in the calf. It pulls against the force of gravity to keep the body upright.

The largest muscle in the body is the gluteus maximus in the butt.

The tongue is not one but sixteen muscles.

The heart has the ability to beat more than one billion times in a life span.

GESUNDHEIT!

Technically speaking, sneezing is called "sternutation."

People don't sneeze in their sleep because the nerves that control sneezing are also at rest.

Most people sneeze through their mouth; animals, through their nose.

One-third of people have a medical condition known as ACHOO (autosomal dominant compelling helio-ophthalmic outburst) syndrome, a genetic condition wherein sunlight stimulates the optic nerves, sending sensory impulses to the trigeminal nerve in the nose, which causes a tickle, resulting in a sneeze.

Instead of saying, "God bless you," after a sneeze, Zulus say, "I am now blessed." Greeks and Romans said, "Banish the omen." Hindus say, "Live," with the response, "With you."

Some people sneeze while plucking their eyebrows since this causes the nerves in the face to fire and affect the nasal nerve.

Your heart doesn't stop when you sneeze, but a change in the pressure in your chest changes your blood flow, which may change the rhythm of your heart.

WEIRD MEDICINE

A nine-year-old Greek girl was found to have her embryonic twin in her abdomen in 2008. Doctors surgically removed the formed two-inch fetus, which had a head, hair, and eyes.

In 2008, doctors in Colorado Springs, Colorado, thought a three-day-old infant had a brain tumor.

Upon operating, they found a fully developed foot, and a partially developed foot, hand, and thigh in the child's brain.

A Michigan woman had a 308-pound ovarian cyst removed in 1951, during a four-day surgical procedure.

The longest any person has ever stayed awake was 264 hours and 12 minutes. The person then slept for fifteen hours.

One in 358 Old Order Mennonite infants have what is called "maple syrup disease," which is characterized by, among other things, urine that has a distinctive sweet odor, similar to burned caramel, or maple syrup.

BAD MEDICINE

The worst time to get a prescription filled is the beginning of the month, when Social Security checks go out and pharmacies are busiest. The first few days of the month are when the most fatal medication errors are made.

Medical mistakes kill almost 98,000 Americans a year.

HAIRY APES

Humans have hair. Animals have fur.

There are three kinds of hair: Lanugo is the fine hair that covers a fetus. Vellus hair is that tiny delicate hair that covers almost the entire body. Terminal hair is the larger more developed hair.

An average head of hair would be able to hold ten to fifteen tons of weight, if the scalp were stronger.

Each hair on the human body grows on its own cycle. Good thing too, since if they grew in synchrony, we would molt!

After thirty years of age, the chance of going gray increases by 10 to 20 percent every decade.

Redheads have a higher incidence of skin cancer.

Blonds have more hair than brunettes, and brunettes more than redheads.

Head lice can change color to blend in with hair.

BODY PARTS

The middle fingernail grows the fastest, the thumbnail the slowest.

Some newborn boys have swollen breasts that can exude a sweet, white fluid known as "witches' milk."

A man once had feet that required special size 29½ shoes.

An adult emits the same energy as a one-hundred-watt lightbulb.

The record distance for projectile vomiting is twenty-seven feet.

The most common time for a heart attack is Monday morning, followed by Saturday morning.

Research reported in the 1992 book *The Left-Handed Syndrome* indicates that left-handed people live about ten years less than right-handers do.

A 2008 study at the Karolinska Institute in Stockholm and Umeå University in northern Sweden found that people with high IQs are better able to keep a beat.

The six basic human facial expressions are happiness, sadness, fear, anger, surprise, and disgust.

WILD THINGS

WHALE'S TALES

Baleen whales have no teeth. They strain their food from the water.

Toothed whales have one blowhole. Baleen whales have two.

A humpback whale calf will drink up to 130 gallons of milk a day.

While nursing her young, a humpback whale mother can go for eight months without eating.

Humpback whales sing songs that last a half hour.

Blue whale vocalizations can be detected more than one thousand miles away underwater.

Sperm whales will emit a sonar blast that can immobilize a squid.

Bowhead whales can live to be two hundred years old.

THEY CALL HIM FLIPPER

Dolphins are toothed whales.

Bottlenose dolphins identify themselves by name when whistling to other dolphins.

Dolphins have been known to risk their own lives to protect humans from sharks in open water.

Besides humans and other primates, only bottlenose dolphins, killer whales, elephants, and European magpies have been found to recognize themselves in a mirror. (Children don't until they are about eighteen months old.)

Bottlenose dolphins can hear sounds in frequencies from 200 to 150,000 Hz. Elephants can hear from 1 to 20,000 Hz. (By comparison, humans can hear from 20 to 20,000 Hz.)

JAWS

The bite of a large white shark is the most powerful of any living species and probably more powerful than that of a dinosaur.

Female tiger sharks have two uteri, and several embryos develop in each. However, only one shark per uterus is born because the dominant one survives by eating the others.

SOMETHING'S FISHY

Hagfish are known as one of the most disgusting creatures in the sea. They can produce seventeen quarts of slippery slime to gross out and confuse would-be predators.

The fastest fish—the sailfish—can achieve a top speed of 69 miles per hour. The seahorse tops out at a more leisurely 0.01 mile per hour.

SONIC GRENADES

By snapping shut its large claw, the pistol shrimp shoots out a jet of water so fast it makes an air bubble that creates a massive shock wave that, when it implodes, is louder than a whale's call. The blast of energy produces light and temperatures near 18,000°F inside the bubble. These "sonic grenades" can kill nearby shrimp or fish.

FLOTSAM AND JETSAM

Young oysters are called spats.

A 405-year-old clam was recently found off the coast of Iceland.

Cyanea arctica, a North Atlantic jellyfish, can have 125-foot-long tentacles.

Octopuses taste things with their tentacles.

Krill are the world's most abundant multicellular animal biomass, by weight.

Tube worms from deep-sea thermal vents can live for 250 years.

Sunflower starfish measure three feet across.

WHAT'S BUGGING YOU?

The world's largest ant colony stretches from Italy to Portugal, some 3,700 miles.

Pharaoh ants are a pest in hospitals, where they are attracted to wounds and bloody bandages. Because of this fondness, they have been known to spread contamination and disease.

Locust swarms can be up to ten miles wide.

Horny cicadas can produce love calls of around 120 decibels, the equivalent of a rock concert or jet engine.

Under favorable conditions, sixty thousand termites can consume a one-foot-long two-by-four in as little as four months.

The atlas moth has a wingspan of almost one foot.

The Queen Alexandra's birdwing butterfly, of Papua, New Guinea, has an eleven-inch wingspan.

The "powder" that comes off a butterfly's wing when touched is really tiny scales. Don't worry though; they can still fly just fine.

The rhinoceros beetle of Southeast Asia can carry 850 times its own weight. That'd be like a human hauling around 130,000 pounds.

Some insects taste with their jaws, antennae, and legs.

Below 37 miles per hour, most bugs tend to bounce off car windshields; above this speed they start to splatter.

◊ WHAT'S THE BUZZ?

Worker honeybees have 5,500 lenses in each eye.

African honeybees kill more people on the African plain than do lions, leopards, or cheetahs. They form swarms of up to thirty thousand and will pursue victims for up to a mile, repeatedly stinging them.

In 1957, a beekeeper in Brazil was trying to cross an African bee with a honeybee to yield a more durable insect for the tropics. Of course, the African bee queens escaped and bred with the local honeybees, creating killer bees. These extremely aggressive Africanized bees have now spread northward into the American Southwest.

The queen bee was called the king bee until the late 1660s, when a Dutch scientist took the time to dissect one.

Australian researchers have found that bees can recognize different human faces.

The Stealthy Insect Sensor Project, at Los Alamos National Laboratory in New Mexico, has trained bees to detect explosives.

One-third of the world's honeybees have recently died for unknown reasons.

 ## SKEETERS

Mosquitoes are the most deadly animals. They transmit diseases such as dengue fever, encephalitis, malaria, yellow fever, and West Nile virus.

Happily, mosquitoes don't transmit HIV. They digest the virus along with their blood meal.

Citronella repels mosquitoes because it irritates their feet.

Mosquitoes are more attracted to blonds than brunettes, and to children more than to adults.

It has been calculated that if you were bitten by 1,120,000 mosquitoes simultaneously, you would be totally drained of your blood.

Only female mosquitoes feed on blood; males are more docile nectar feeders.

A new species of mosquito has evolved in the London Underground from ones that flew in there when the tunnels were dug a hundred years ago.

A chemical signal tells a mosquito when it is full, so it will stop feeding. This signal has been disabled in lab tests and the skeeters sucked blood until they exploded.

Komarno, Manitoba, is the self-proclaimed mosquito capital of Canada.

🐚 STING OPERATION

Young scorpions are called scorplings.

The mother scorpion carries her scorplings around on her back until they are able to fend for themselves.

Scorpions glow in the dark under black light. This makes finding them at night easy.

Forty different scorpion species have venom strong enough to kill a human.

Bigger scorpions tend to be less venomous than smaller ones.

🐚 WEBMASTERS

Some spiders mimic bird poop to avoid being eaten by birds while resting on a leaf.

Goliath bird-eater tarantulas are as big as a dinner plate and, as the name implies, can eat birds.

Spiders can produce seven kinds of silk, some stiff and strong, others sticky and elastic.

FOR THE BIRDS

The African red-billed queleas are the most numerous birds in the world. A flock may take up to five hours to pass overhead.

Cave swiftlets navigate in the dark by making click-ing sounds, much like bats do.

It takes cave swiftlets thirty days to make their nests, entirely out of saliva.

Antarctic petrels have to fly six hundred miles round trip to bring food from the sea to their young.

Oxpeckers, African birds similar to starlings, eat ticks, scabs, blood, earwax, and dandruff from large mammals.

A hawk's vision is 20/5. It can see from twenty feet what a human can see from five feet.

Domesticated turkeys are bred with white feathers so as not to discolor the skin.

The long, red fleshy growth that hangs down over the neck at the base of a turkey's beak is the snood. The red or pink fleshy growth on top of the head is the caruncle, and the bright red appendage on the neck is the wattle.

Many birds use gravity to swallow, so there won't be any birds on space missions.

There are six species of poisonous birds in New Guinea. They have neurotoxins in their leg feathers, breast, and belly.

"Mike the Wonder Chicken" was a bird who had his head chopped off (but not his brain stem), and still lived for almost two more years. He toured America and was fed with an eyedropper directly into his gullet.

A hummingbird's heart beats 1,260 times per minute in flight, and it needs to consume more than its own body weight each day to survive. Thus, at any given time, a hummingbird is only hours from starvation.

Young hawks are called eyas. Young hens are known as pullets and young roosters as cockerels. Young pigeons are squabs.

A group of geese on the ground is a gaggle. A group of geese in the air is a skein.

The reason geese poop everywhere is because they can't digest food fast enough to enable them to fly after eating.

Ostriches blink once per minute, compared to parrots, which blink twenty-six times.

The cuckoo bird lays her eggs in the nests of unsuspecting warblers (after knocking one of their eggs out of the nest), which raise the cuckoo chicks as their own. For some reason, the warbler mom isn't bothered by the fact that the cuckoo chick rapidly grows to ten times her own size.

Bald eagles once built a nest nearly ten feet wide and twenty feet deep near St. Petersburg, Florida.

The bee hummingbird of Cuba only weighs 1.6 grams.

The heaviest bird that can fly is the forty-nine-pound mute swan.

The arctic tern flies about twenty-four thousand miles round trip on its migration from the Arctic to Antarctica.

The American woodcock can remain airborne at just 5 miles per hour.

The male emperor penguin incubates the egg in his brood pouch for sixty-five days before it hatches. Then he secretes a white milky substance from the same pouch to feed the chick.

Some penguins live near the equator on the Galapagos Islands.

NATURE'S GARBAGE MEN

Vultures can eat meat containing, anthrax, botulism, and cholera.

Vultures can't sweat, so they pee on their legs to cool off.

A Ruppell's vulture was once recorded flying at a height of 37,000 feet, just before it crashed into an airliner over the Ivory Coast.

KILLER CONSERVATION

Ornithologist and naturalist John James Audubon killed thousands of birds as subjects for his incredibly accurate and lifelike paintings.

I VANT TO SUCK YOUR BLOOD

Vampire bats are only the size of a thumb. They open a vein with their razor-sharp teeth and will drink up to five teaspoons of blood in one meal. Fear not, they prefer cows to people.

Vampire bats begin urinating as soon as they start feeding.

Bats must eat every day or die.

A hungry bat will flick the cheek of a full bat, causing it to vomit up blood, which the hungry bat eagerly scarfs up.

Bats are not blind, but do have weak eyesight, so they use echolocation to navigate.

When bats are flying around in a cave getting ready to leave for the night, they ignore their echolocation system because the thousands of other bats around them make a chaotic noise. If you wandered into the cave at this time, they would crash into you.

Bats with bigger testes have smaller brains (like another species we know).

There is a three-hundred-foot-deep pile of guano (bat poop) in a cave in Borneo.

SLITHERIN'

The snake with the most deadly venom is the inland, or western taipan, found near Queensland, Australia. Its venom is fifty times stronger than the king cobra's.

A dead rattlesnake can still bite for several hours, even if the head is separated from the body.

One hundred thousand people die from snakebites each year in Asia.

In the United States, more people die from bee and wasp stings than snakebites.

The bite of a mamba is lethal almost 100 percent of the time.

King cobras mainly eat other snakes.

Cobras are deaf. It's not the music of the snake charmer that fascinates them, but the movement of the flute.

The heat-sensitive organ between a rattlesnake's eyes can detect thermal changes as little as 0.0036°F.

Reticulated pythons can grow to thirty-two feet.

UDDERLY ESSENTIAL

Cows are designed to feed on grass, not grain, so when they eat grain they get indigestion. Half of the baking soda sold in the United States is used to calm cow indigestion.

Cows can produce one half gallon of methane gas per minute, contributing to global warming.

MEMORY LIKE AN ELEPHANT

Separated mother and daughter elephants have remembered each other after twenty-three years apart.

Elephants can retain a mental map of their entire home range, an area that can be the size of Rhode Island.

Both sexes of African elephants grow tusks. Typically, only male Asian elephants do so.

Elephants use their trunks to resonate the twenty-five different sounds they make. Elephants can communicate over long distances using ultra-low-frequency infrasound, which can be detected by other elephants several miles away through the skin in their feet and trunk.

Zoologists estimate elephants kill five hundred people a year.

Elephants and rabbits have big ears to facilitate heat loss.

Elephants are excellent swimmers. Experts believe they

once swam from southern India to Sri Lanka, where they settled.

IN COLD BLOOD

Frogs, lizards, lampreys, and some fish have a parietal, or third, "eye" on their foreheads, which is a patch of skin that is photosensitive and helps control their circadian rhythms.

A chameleon's tongue is twice its body length.

Some chameleons turn red when angry.

Salamanders make no sounds and can hear no sounds.

Chinese giant salamanders have been known to reach a length of six feet and live for eighty years.

There are no male whiptail lizards. Females will produce enough testosterone to mimic male behavior (mounting another female), causing other females to lay and fertilize their own eggs.

The male Surinam toad pushes eggs into the back of the female toad, where they become embedded. The eggs hatch there in pockets under her skin and develop into fully formed toads before emerging.

ATTACK OF THE GIANT ANTEATER

Anteaters are the only mammals without any teeth.

Giant anteaters flick their tongues in and out up to 150 times a minute while feeding and can eat up thirty thousand insects a day.

In 2007, a giant anteater at a zoo in Buenos Aires attacked and killed its nineteen-year-old keeper.

PRIMARY PRIMATES

Chimps have better short-term memory than humans.

Chimps are cannibals.

Chimps have better short-term memory than humans. (Get it?)

New World monkeys have "fingerprints" on the underside of their tails to help them grip better.

Orangutans usually build a new nest of branches and leaves high up in the trees every night.

Orangutan babies nurse for up to six years.

Baboons eat hippo dung.

The pygmy mouse lemur is the smallest primate, weighing only one ounce.

Slow lorises secrete a toxin from inside their elbows that they then suck into their mouths and lick onto their young to protect them when left alone.

LE PEW

Skunks will eat anything that moves, including live bees and bats.

Skunk spray is highly flammable.

Rattlesnakes are afraid of skunks.

In populated areas, cars are the leading killer of skunks.

Some people keep skunks as pets. Pet skunks come in many colors, including white, blond, and lavender.

WALKING PINCUSHIONS

Porcupine quills are naturally antiseptic. This is a good thing, as porcupines often impale other porcupines and themselves.

The porcupine male urinates on the female to get her attention.

SQUIGGLY WIGGLIES

Blood fluke worms can live in the bladder for up to thirty years. They lay spiny eggs that rupture the bladder wall.

One in four people worldwide have roundworms in their stomachs.

There's an earthworm (*Megascilides australis*) in Australia that grows ten feet long, with a diameter of one inch.

Earthworms taste with their entire body.

RATS!

Rats must constantly gnaw things to wear down their teeth, which grow up to five and a half inches a year.

Rats have been known to survive being flushed down the toilet. Some even have returned to the toilet via the plumbing.

Karni Mata is a Hindu temple in India overrun with thousands of rats, but this is okay since the Hindus worship them.

Rat baiting was a popular sport in England in the nineteenth century. A thirteen-pound bull terrier holds the record of having killed one hundred rats in five minutes and twenty-eight seconds in 1862.

The reason rats have no fur on their tails is because they do not sweat, but cool off by expanding or contracting the blood vessels in their tails.

Four million years ago, there were rats the size of bulls.

In a rat colony, the higher-ranking rats live nearer the food.

Mother rats will eat their babies if food is in short supply.

Rats destroy $19 billion worth of stored grains each year in the United States.

Some shrews will eat three times their body weight each day.

The pygmy shrew, at 1.3 grams, is the lightest mammal.

Some shrews have a venomous bite.

WATER RATS

Otters' fur is so dense that water never touches their skin.

A busy beaver can chew through a five-inch-diameter willow tree in three minutes. A pair will fell four hundred trees in a year.

HOORAY FOR HIPPOS

Hippos sleep underwater and automatically surface every few minutes to breathe. They only come out of the water to feed on grass.

Male hippos have the habit while defecating of spinning their tails to spread their excrement about to attract females.

Hippos can be very violent and are considered the most dangerous large animal in Africa, often killing people.

They may resemble pigs, but hippos are genetically closer to whales.

Hippos, like pigs, can sunburn, so to protect themselves they secrete a natural thick, red-colored mucus sunscreen called "blood sweat."

TALL TALES

The blue black color of a giraffe's tongue may be to keep it from getting sunburned while feeding.

Giraffes clean out their noses with their eighteen-inch tongue. They also are profuse droolers.

Giraffe meat and milk are kosher.

Giraffes have the same number of vertebrae as other mammals—seven—they are just much more elongated.

Giraffes are one of the few animals born with horns.

GREAT GATORS

You can tell an alligator from a crocodile by its U-shaped snout. Crocs have V-shaped snouts.

Saltwater crocodiles can be up to twenty-three feet long.

Alligator eggs that are incubated at temperatures of 90 to 93°F will be male. Temperatures of 82 to 86°F result in females. Intermediate temps yield a mix of males and females.

ROCKY MOUNTAIN OYSTERS

A champion bull's sperm may be worth up to $150,000 and he may father one hundred thousand offspring.

> The bigger a bull's testicles, the more likely he will be used for breeding; the smaller boys, as it were, will be castrated.

Castrated bull's testicles are breaded and fried to make a dish known as Rocky Mountain oysters.

> Bulls are color-blind. It is not the color red that angers them in a bullfight, but the movements of the cape. The capes are red to hide any blood they get on them.

LIONS AND TIGERS AND . . .

The panda is one bear that doesn't hibernate. Its meager diet of bamboo leaves isn't nutritious enough for it to store the fat needed to sleep through the winter.

> Polar bears have been found swimming in the Arctic Ocean two hundred miles from land. They swim at 6 miles per hour.

A female polar bear needs to gain at least 440 pounds

for a successful pregnancy. If her fat content is not high enough, her body will reabsorb the fetus.

A lion's mane is his calling card to the ladies. A lighter color indicates a well-fed, parasite-free male. Darker manes cause the lion's body temperature to rise in the sun, reducing sperm count.

IMPOSTERS

Koalas are not bears, but marsupials.

Koala babies consume mom's poop to acquire the bacteria needed to detoxify the poison in the eucalyptus leaves they eat.

Koalas have fingerprints almost identical to humans. You need an electron microscope to tell them apart.

Koalas sleep nineteen to twenty-two hours a day. (Good work if you can get it.)

Male koalas have a two-headed penis and the females have two vaginas.

PLAYING POSSUM

When opossums play dead, they pass out, foam at the mouth, stick their tongues out, excrete on themselves, and ooze a nasty green slime from their anus that smells like rotting flesh.

Kangaroos lick saliva onto their forearms to keep cool.

Tasmanian devils can eat 40 percent of their own body weight in thirty minutes.

WHAT IS IT?

The platypus has bird, mammal, and reptile genome features, although it is still classified as a mammal.

The male platypus is one of the few venomous mammals. It has a spur on its hind foot that can deliver painful venom.

HOOVER HOGS

The nine-banded armadillo, the only armadillo species found in the United States, can jump four feet straight up into the air when startled. The only problem is, it tends to do so as vehicles are passing over it, and get killed by the undercarriage.

Armadillos can walk across the bottom of a body of water or inflate their intestines with air and float across.

In Texas, armadillos were known as "Hoover hogs" during the Great Depression, when they were hunted for food.

ON THE BRINK

The United States has the greatest number of threatened species—935.

About one-third of amphibians are endangered, more than any other group of animal.

The alligator was removed from the list of threatened and endangered U.S. species in 1987 and has since become quite a nuisance in its home range.

Some other notable recovered species removed from the list include the gray whale (1994), the brown pelican (1985), the American peregrine falcon (1999), the Arctic peregrine falcon (1994), the bald eagle (2007), and the northern Rocky Mountain gray wolf (2008).

Sadly, the Samson's pearly mussel, the tecopa pupfish, the blue pike, the dusky seaside sparrow, and the Santa Barbara song sparrow also have all been removed from the list, because they are now extinct.

Hawaii tops the list of threatened or endangered species in one state with 329.

Hawaii's po'ouli is the rarest bird in the world. Only two are known to remain.

The rarest mammal is the Yangtze River dolphin; only around twenty are known.

The Vancouver Island marmot is the rarest land mammal, with about twenty-nine left. There are about sixty Javan rhinoceroses alive today.

"Lonesome George," the last surviving Pinta Island tortoise of the Galápagos Islands, is the rarest creature in the world.

ALMOST HUMAN

Very few vertebrates mate face-to-face like humans. Those that do include beavers, bonobos, hamsters, and orangutans.

The only other species besides humans that French kiss is the white-fronted parrot. After they touch tongues, the male vomits on the female's chest. (How romantic.)

STUDS AND DUDS

The male paper nautilus octopus's penis detaches and swims to the female to impregnate her.

The male spiny anteater has a four-headed penis. Only two fit into the female at one time.

The male penguin has one orgasm a year.

Most male birds have no penis.

The raccoon penis has a little bone in it that was once used as a toothpick.

The female Barbary macaque must yell in order to get the male to ejaculate.

Male snakes have two penises with barbs to lock into the female and mate for eight to twelve hours.

A gorilla's penis is a mere two inches long.

The penis of the male Argentine lake duck is corkscrewed and 42.5 centimeters long, longer than the duck itself. Most impressive.

A dog's penis has a knotlike structure on the end that locks the male into the female, a phenomenon known as penis-captivus.

The northern right whale has testes that weigh eleven hundred pounds each.

Fruit flies have the biggest sperm relative to body size—two-thirds of an inch long—three hundred times bigger than human sperm.

GETTING IT ON

Porpoises engage in group sex.

Chimps don't engage in foreplay, and copulation lasts about three seconds.

Minks can do it for up to eight hours at a clip.

Pandas are notoriously hard to breed in captivity, so in China they give the males Viagra. Now the male can go from previously lasting thirty seconds to lasting twenty minutes.

When the pandas reach adulthood, Chinese zookeepers even show them films of other pandas doing it, to give them the idea.

Mosquitoes mate for two seconds, in midair.

Hamsters and gerbils can copulate one hundred times in an hour.

Generally speaking, wild animals don't get VD.

The female snake can store sperm for years until it's needed.

GAY KINGDOM

More than fifteen hundred different species exhibit homosexual behavior.

Male giraffes are bisexual, and 94 percent of copulations are between two males.

Turkeys are also bisexual.

Seagulls sometimes engage in lesbian mating, resulting in sterile eggs.

A female goose may get in on the act with two romancing homosexual male geese and copulate with both. Both males will then help parent the young.

THE SECRET LIFE OF PLANTS

GREEN GIANTS

The stinking corpse lily (*Rafflesia*) flower measures up to thirty-nine inches in diameter and reeks of rotting meat to attract the carrion flies it needs for pollination.

The Victoria giant water lily has floating leaves that are big enough to support a small child.

The African raffia palm has leaves up to eighty feet long.

The heaviest organism is probably the "Pando" stand of quaking aspen clones in Utah, all part of the same root system and genetically identical, weighing in the neighborhood of 6,600 tons.

The largest alga is the giant kelp of the California coast that can reach lengths of 177 feet.

The tallest tree ever was not a redwood, but an Australian eucalyptus that measured 435 feet when it fell over in 1872. Its top had previously broken off and is believed to have been almost 500 feet at one time.

Grasses cover more of Earth than any other plant, and feed the most animals.

HEARTS AND FLOWERS

There are no perfectly pure black flowers.

Scientists have engineered an orchid that glows in the dark.

Sea grass is the only flowering plant found in the oceans.

Goldenrod does not cause hay fever. It gets the blame because its showy yellow flowers bloom around the same time as the inconspicuous green flowers of the true culprit—ragweed.

Fig tree flowers are found *inside* the fruit.

Although tulips today are associated with Holland, they originated in the Persian Empire.

There are only two flowering plants native to Antarctica.

Evening primrose flowers open at dusk and close at dawn. They rely on moths for pollination.

The colorful red part of a poinsettia that most people think is the flower is really a number of bracts (modified leaves). The flower is the little yellow center part.

The poinsettia was brought to the United States from Mexico in 1829 by Joel R. Poinsett, the U.S. ambassador to that country.

Saffron comes from the stigma (female part that receives the pollen) of crocus flowers.

It requires fifty to seventy-five thousand crocus flowers to make a pound of dried saffron.

A ROSE IS A ROSE

The American Rose Society lists more than sixteen thousand rose varieties in its current reference book.

There are no true blue roses.

SEEDY SIDE OF PLANTS

Some oaks produce acorns when twenty years old, others not till they are fifty years old.

A strawberry is the only fruit with the seeds on the outside. Botanically speaking, those little "seeds" on the outside are actually the fruits, not the red "berry." Tiny seeds are found inside these little fruits.

Wild rice isn't rice at all, but the brown seed of an aquatic grass plant native to North America.

A two-thousand-year-old date seed was recently germinated and grown into an adult plant.

Ricin, from the seeds of the castor bean, is probably the most deadly plant toxin—0.00002 ounces is enough to kill a human.

Ferdinand von Mueller, director of the Royal Botanical Gardens in Australia, discovered the macadamia nut in 1858 and named it in honor of his friend, John Macadam, secretary of the Philosophical Institute of Victoria.

Hundreds of miles above the Arctic Circle, in Spitsbergen, Norway, is something called the "Doomsday Vault," a seed depository that can withstand any natural disaster or even a nuclear attack. Hundreds of thousands of plant seeds from all over the world are stored there, to repopulate the planet in case a species is wiped out by disease or disaster.

FRUITY FACTS

The fig is the sweetest fruit.

The mango is the most popular fruit in the world.

The word "avocado" is derived from the Aztec word *ahuacatl*, which means "testicle." Take a good look at an avocado and you'll see why.

APPLES TO APPLES

Red Delicious and Golden Delicious apples are not related to each other but *were* marketed by the same person.

Apple trees do not reproduce true from seed. Apple seedlings don't inherit exact copies of their parents' DNA, and thus do not resemble them. Seeds from an apple can produce trees with entirely different fruit. For this reason, apple trees are always grafted, to maintain true varieties.

All the McIntosh apples in the world come from the grafting of one tree found by John McIntosh in an abandoned Ontario apple orchard in 1811.

The Granny Smith apple was discovered by a chance seed planted by Maria Ann Smith of Australia in 1868. It was introduced to the United States in 1972.

KICK IT UP A NOTCH!

Chili peppers are hot to prevent fungi from growing on wounds caused by feeding insects. Birds and insects are not affected by the pepper's "heat."

The only three spices native to the New World are vanilla, allspice, and chili peppers.

Mace and nutmeg come from the fruit of the same plant.

Nutmeg, in large quantities, can produce hallucinations and euphoria. (Its other side effects are extremely dangerous, though.)

REEFER MADNESS

Marijuana is the leading cash crop in the United States, worth more than the annual corn and wheat crops combined.

If pot were legalized, the United States could save nearly $8 billion a year in enforcement costs and rake in $7 billion in taxes.

Pot is the most widely used illegal drug. About 40 percent of Americans say they have tried it.

The amount of THC found in marijuana today is two to three times what it was a decade ago.

Newer varieties of pot are more likely to cause psychotic episodes, due to a lack of the moderating chemical cannabidiol.

Only 9 percent of pot smokers become dependent, compared with 15 percent of alcohol drinkers, 17 percent of cocaine users, 23 percent of heroin users, and 32 percent of tobacco smokers.

There are only two documented cases of someone dying from an overdose of marijuana. This compares with two hundred thousand a year from other illegal drugs, 2.5 million from alcohol, and 5 million from long-term effects of smoking tobacco.

GREATEST MAN WHO EVER LIVED

American plant breeder Norman Borlaug may be the most important person who ever lived. During the mid-twentieth century, he developed higher-yielding, disease-resistant grains and introduced modern farming techniques to numerous Third World countries, saving an estimated 1 billion people from death by starvation. Oh, yes, he won the Nobel Prize for Peace in 1970.

KERNELS OF KNOWLEDGE

An ear of corn is a cluster of female flowers. The silks are elongated stigmas— the tubes that the pollen grows down to fertilize the ovaries and create the kernels (fruits).

There are about 625 carnivorous plant species.

Bristlecone pines live for up to five thousand years.

Moss grows on the north side of trees because this is the side that gets the least sunlight and remains dampest.

Algae produce three-quarters of the oxygen found in the atmosphere.

The leaves of certain *Mimosa* species display thigmonasty—they close up immediately when touched or from rapid changes in temperature.

The leaves of the silk tree (also known as mimosa) slowly close up at nighttime or during rainy weather.

GAMES PEOPLE PLAY

TOSSIN' AROUND THE OLD PIGSKIN

Rutgers College and what is now Princeton University played the first intercollegiate football game in New Brunswick, New Jersey, on November 6, 1869. Rutgers won 6–4. (The scoring was different back then.)

In 1873, there were fifteen players on a football team.

A system of downs wasn't introduced until Walter Camp did so in 1882. At first, it was three downs to get five yards. Then in 1906, they upped it to ten yards. A fourth down was added in 1912.

The system of downs was introduced because in an 1881 game between unbeaten Yale and Harvard, neither team tried to advance the ball, so that they could remain unbeaten.

Early college football was so brutal that by 1905, eighteen

players had died, prompting Teddy Roosevelt to call for reforms. The National Collegiate Athletic Association (NCAA) was formed. They introduced the forward pass and shortened the games from seventy to sixty minutes.

> The first legal forward pass took place in a 1905 game between St. Louis University and Carroll College (Wisconsin).

Before 1933, an NFL pass had to be attempted from five yards behind the line of scrimmage.

> In 1912, the points awarded for a touchdown were increased from five to six.

The two-point conversion was added to college football in 1958 and to the NFL in 1994.

> In 1935, Fordham football player Ed Smith modeled for the Heisman Trophy, which was named for the first director of New York's Downtown Athletic Club—John W. Heisman—who died in 1936.

RAH! RAH!

The first cheerleaders were male. Johnny Campbell, of the University of Minnesota, led the first cheer at a football game, in 1898. The university still uses his original cheer today.

Women weren't allowed to cheer until 1923.

GOOD SPORTS, BAD SPORTS

In a 1940 Cornell–Dartmouth football game, Cornell won on a last-second illegal fifth down play. After reviewing the game film two days later, the Cornell coach realized the error and called the Dartmouth coach to forfeit the game. (Classy.)

In a similar 1990 game between Colorado and Missouri, the officials inadvertently gave Colorado a fifth down and the Buffaloes scored a last-second touchdown to win the game. Referee J. C. Louderback was made aware of the error before Colorado kicked the extra point, but after a twenty-minute discussion he decided to let the play stand. The Colorado coach took the win. (Not so classy.)

LET'S GO TO THE VIDEO

Instant replay was first used by CBS in 1963, during the Army-Navy football game. It was invented by CBS sports director Tony Verna. So as not to totally confuse viewers, announcer Lindsey Nelson had to keep screaming, "This is a videotape. They did not score again! They did not score again!"

THE GREATEST GAME
EVER PLAYED

The 1958 Colts–Giants NFL Championship Game, known as the "Greatest Game Ever Played," was blacked out in the New York market because it was being played at Yankee Stadium.

During the sudden-death overtime, a spectator accidentally kicked out NBC's power cable, and television sets across the nation went blank at the climax of the game. A quick-thinking NBC crew member ran out onto the field to disrupt the game, as police chased him around the field. This gave NBC time to reconnect the cable, and the folks at home only missed one play.

An easel with flash cards was used during the telecast for down and distance.

NFL game telecasts back then had no pregame or postgame shows and no tapes were kept of the games.

No network footage of Super Bowl I exists today. Legend has it that the game was taped over for a soap opera.

BRETT REGRET

The Atlanta Falcons drafted Brett Favre in 1991. Coach Jerry Glanville disapproved of Favre and said it would take a "plane crash" before he'd play him. Favre went on to set the NFL records for most touchdowns, yards, completions, attempts, interceptions, and consecutive games by a quarterback, and also won three MVP awards.

The first pass of Brett Favre's NFL career was an interception returned for a touchdown, when he played for the Atlanta Falcons in 1991. He completed no passes with the Falcons.

Favre's first NFL completion was to himself for a seven-yard loss, in his first game as a Green Bay Packer.

HE GOES BOTH WAYS

In 1943, Sammy Baugh of the Washington Redskins was a three-way player. He led the NFL in passing yards, punting yards, and interceptions. In one game he threw four touchdowns on offense and intercepted four passes on defense.

PIRATES AND INDIANS

The Pittsburgh Pirates were originally the Alleghenys. They picked up their current name when, in 1891, they "stole" a player from the Philadelphia Athletics and were labeled as "pirates." To make sport of the derogatory nickname, they adopted it as their own.

The Cleveland Indians chose their name to honor a Native American—Louis Sockalexis— who briefly played for the team, the first "Indian" to play professional baseball. Earlier names for the team included the Lake Shores, the Forest Citys, the Blues, the Broncos, and the Spiders.

The L.A. Dodgers came from Brooklyn, where Manhattanites referred to Brooklynites as "trolley dodgers," because of all the trolley cars there at the time. Other names in their history included the Atlantics, the Grays, the Bridegrooms, the Grooms, the Superbas, and the Robins.

The Chicago Cubs were known as the White Stockings, Colts, and Orphans in the late nineteenth century. They came by their current name in 1902. After they had signed several young players, a local newspaper penned the nickname "Cubs."

The New York Yankees were first called the Highlanders and Hilltoppers.

The Boston Red Sox were known as the Americans, Pilgrims, Puritans, Plymouth Rocks, and Somersets at various times in their early history.

The Los Angeles Lakers were originally from Minneapolis, the "Land of 10,000 Lakes." They kept the name "Lakers" when they moved to L.A.

The New York Knicks get their name from Washington Irving's *History of New York*, a story that made fun of the Dutch settlers of New York City, which he wrote under the pseudonym Diedrich Knickerbocker.

The Buffalo Bills logo is actually a bison. No buffaloes *or* bison ever lived there.

Barron Hilton, heir to the Hilton Hotel fortune and president of the Carte Blanche credit card company, named his San Diego football team the "Chargers," as a nod to credit cards and because it sounded exciting.

The Green Bay Packers took their name from the Indian

Packing Company that supplied the team with equipment and a field in their first year.

In 1943, the Pittsburgh Steelers and the Philadelphia Eagles merged for the season because both teams had lost so many players to the war, becoming the Steagles.

The Kansas City Chiefs claim their name honors ex-mayor Roe Bartle, nicknamed "the Chief." Prior to 1963, they were the Dallas Texans.

FREE THROWS

The first basketball game, played in a Springfield, Massachusetts, YMCA in 1891, ended with a 1–0 score.

Early basketball used intact peach baskets, and the ball had to be retrieved from the basket after each score.

Metal hoops and a backboard were added in 1906.

YMCA teams from Trenton, New Jersey, and Brooklyn, New York, played the first professional basketball game at the Trenton Masonic Lodge in 1896. Trenton won 15–1.

The twenty-four-second shot clock was introduced to the NBA in 1954 to increase scoring. The three-point shot was added in 1980.

In 1950, blacks were allowed into the NBA for the first time.

Robert Parish holds the NBA record for games played, with 1,611.

In 1993, Michael Williams, of the NBA Minnesota Timberwolves, sank ninety-three consecutive free throws.

"Pistol" Pete Maravich holds the NCAA record for points scored in a college career—3,677.

OUT IN THE COLD

Scandinavians strapped the shinbones of cattle and sheep to the bottoms of their boots thirteen hundred years ago to fashion the first ice skates.

Figure skating began in eighteenth-century Scottish skating clubs, where members had to jump over hats and trace figures or write names in the ice with their skates.

Frick and Frack were Swiss comedic ice skaters who joined the Ice Follies in 1937.

There are some unique terms for jumps used in figure skating, many named after their inventor:

Axel—first performed in an 1882 competition by Austrian Axel Paulsen in Vienna

Salchow—invented by Swedish skater Ulrich Salchow in 1909

Lutz—invented and first performed by Austrian Alois Lutz in 1913

Olympic gold medal figure skater Kristi Yamaguchi had clubfeet as a child and started skating as a form of therapy.

In the sport of speed skiing competitors can top 155 miles per hour.

IT'S IN THE HOLE!

The average golfer loses 1.8 balls per eighteen holes played. Each year golfers go through some 2.5 billion balls.

Just one-tenth of 1 percent of male golfers shoot par consistently.

Twenty-two-year-old Curt Hocker of El Paso, Texas, got five holes in one in one week on a regulation golf course, and eight total for the year in 2008. The odds of a hole in one are roughly 45,000 to one.

Early on, St. Andrew's golf course in Scotland had just nine holes. The game became so popular in the 1850s that they split each of their fairways in half, longitudinally, and thus created eighteen holes.

Early Scottish golf courses were located near the coast, among sandy dunes. Sheep would gather in the depressions to find shelter from the wind and grazed these spots down to sand—and the first golf bunkers were born.

The term "birdie," for one under par, comes from a hole played by three golfers at the Atlantic City

Country Club in 1899. One of the players' balls hit a bird in flight on his second shot and landed inches from the cup. He putted in on his third shot on the par-4 hole.

Miniature golf was invented in 1926.

TAKE ME OUT TO THE BALLGAME

Jack Norworth wrote the song "Take Me Out to the Ballgame" in 1908. Ironically, he didn't go to his first baseball game until 1940.

The youngest player in the history of Major League Baseball was Joe Nuxhall, who pitched for the Cincinnati Reds at the age of fifteen, in 1944.

The first woman to play professional baseball was Lizzie Arlington, who pitched one game for Reading, Pennsylvania's team against rival Allentown in 1898.

In 1931, an AA professional baseball team—the Chattanooga Lookouts—signed a seventeen-year-old girl—Jackie Mitchell—as a pitcher. In her first appearance, she struck out Babe Ruth and Lou Gehrig in consecutive at-bats. A few days later, baseball commissioner Kenesaw Mountain Landis voided her contract, claiming baseball was "too strenuous" for women.

The first Little League baseball game was played in 1939 in Williamsport, Pennsylvania, home of the Little League World Series.

Strikeouts are called "Ks" because in the 1860s, a batter who whiffed was said to have "struck." When the box score was invented by Henry Chadwick in 1880, "S" was used for a sacrifice, so he took the last letter in "struck" to represent a strikeout.

Major League Baseball didn't require batting helmets until 1971.

Philadelphia Athletics player Doc Powers crashed into an outfield wall on Opening Day, April 12, 1909, attempting to catch a pop-up, developed gangrene, and died from his injuries two weeks later.

SLAP SHOTS

In its inaugural season of 1917–18, the National Hockey League (NHL) made it legal for the first time for goalies to dive on the ice to make a save. This practice would have drawn a penalty before this.

In 1927, the NHL went from two 30-minute halves, to three 20-minute periods.

In 1979, L.A. Kings defenseman Randy Hold received sixty-seven penalty minutes in the first period, making him the only NHL player to ever have more penalty minutes than there is time in a game.

The Stanley Cup, the NHL's championship trophy, is passed along each year with the names of the winning team players and personnel inscribed on it.

The Cup was donated by Lord Stanley Preston, the governor general of Canada, in 1892, as the Dominion Hockey Challenge Cup, to Canada's top amateur hockey club. The original cup was just a little over seven inches tall. Today, it is thirty-five inches high.

SWIFTER, HIGHER, STRONGER

At the 1900 Paris Olympic Games, they held a two-hundred-meter obstacle swim, where swimmers had to swim under and climb over poles and boats. There was also an underwater swim that awarded one point for each second underwater and two points for each meter swum.

The 1904 St. Louis Olympic Games had a plunge-for-distance event, where swimmers dove into the pool and went as far as possible without further propelling themselves or breathing.

Figure skating was originally competed in the 1908 Summer Olympics in London.

Ice hockey debuted at the 1920 Summer Olympics in Antwerp.

Wilma Rudolph was the twentieth child of twenty-two and couldn't walk without braces as a child, due to polio. At the 1960 Rome Olympics, she won three gold medals in sprinting.

NOT QUITE THE OLYMPICS

In the early Scottish Highland Games, competitors were required to twist the four legs off a cow as a test of strength, for which a fat sheep was offered as a prize.

JUST KEEP TURNING LEFT

NASCAR had its roots in the fast, modified cars used by "moonshiners" to outrun the law in the rural South. These drivers began to race one another for bragging rights and cash.

Junior Johnson, a notorious North Carolina moonshiner, who never got caught by the police while behind the wheel, was one NASCAR's biggest early stars. He introduced the tactic of "drafting" to the sport at the 1960 Daytona 500, which he won.

The first woman NASCAR driver was Sara Christian, who raced at the Charlotte Fairgrounds Speedway in 1949.

The only black driver to win a NASCAR race was Wendell Scott in 1963. Because he was black, they announced the second-place finisher the winner. Later, after an official protest, Scott was named the winner, although he never got the trophy.

DADDY NEEDS A
NEW PAIR OF SHOES

Lotteries used to be banned in all fifty states.

New Hampshire, by tying its lottery to horse racing, which was legal, became the first state since the end of the 1800s to have one, in 1964.

In a 2005 Powerball drawing, eighty-nine people picked five out of the six numbers and twenty-one picked six out of six. The odds of this happening are astronomical. Officials discovered the players had all gotten their numbers from fortune cookies that had five of the six numbers.

Foxwoods, owned by the Mashantucket Pequot tribal nation in Connecticut, is the second biggest casino in the world. Only the Venetian in Macau, China, is bigger.

The United States is the only country where roulette wheels have a double zero.

A British man won 500,000 pounds on a thirty-pence accumulator bet by correctly picking the winners in fifteen different sporting events.

All Thoroughbred horses today descend from three stallions brought to England from Arabia in the late 1600s and early 1700s.

Legendary jockey Eddie Araro lost his first 250 races. He went on to ride 4,779 winners.

TOYS "R" US

Silly Putty was the fastest selling toy in history when it debuted in 1949.

The original Wiffle ball bats were made of wood.

The Slinky got its name in 1943, from the wife of its inventor, who saw the Swedish word *slink*, meaning "stealthy, sleek, and sinuous," in a dictionary.

Shia law, in some parts of the world, forbids playing chess and flying kites.

The highest-point word score ever in a Scrabble tournament was 392 points for the word "caziques," the plural for a Caribbean tribal leader or an oriole of the American tropics.

The LEGO toy company was founded in 1934 by a Danish carpenter—Ole Kirk Christiansen—who got the name from the Danish *leg godt*, meaning "play well." He later found out that *lego* also means "I put together" in Latin. The LEGO brick was introduced in 1949.

Play-Doh was originally a wallpaper-cleaning product.

If Barbie were life-size, she would be too skinny to menstruate.

Barbie was modeled after a German sex doll named Lilli.

PONG ANYONE?

The first video game—*Tennis for Two*—was created in 1958. It was played on an oscilloscope and was used to entertain visitors to the Brookhaven National Laboratory on Long Island, New York.

The first computer game—*Spacewar!*—was created to demonstrate the power of MIT's new computer in 1962.

The first home console game system for the television was 1972's Odyssey, by Magnovox.

The song "Pac-Man Fever" made it to number nine on the Billboard charts in 1984.

Space Invaders was so popular in Japan that it caused a nationwide coin shortage.

The Sims is the bestselling PC game of all time.

Up to ten people a week are hospitalized in Britain from injuries suffered while playing Wii games.

UPS AND DOWNS

The original roller coasters were called "Russian Mountains." Built in the 1600s around St. Petersburg, they were sled rides that consisted of ice-covered hills of seventy to eighty feet, with fifty-degree drops.

The first wheeled roller coaster on a track, inspired by Russian Mountains, was built in Paris in 1804.

George Ferris built the first Ferris wheel, for the 1893 Chicago World's Fair.

OVERTIME

Volleyball was invented as a game for older businessmen in 1895 at the Holyoke, Massachusetts, YMCA.

The world record for stone skipping is fifty-one skips.

Before clay pigeons were introduced in 1880, skeet and trap shooters shot at glass targets.

Early Ping-Pong rackets were made of parchment stretched over a frame, which made a "ping-pong" sound when hit.

In 1970, 127 runners competed in the New York City Marathon. Now the field has to be limited to 37,000.

In the 650, or so, matches each year at Wimbledon, around 42,000 balls are used.

A study published in *Psychological Science* found that among evenly matched sporting competitors, wearing red can give one opponent an edge, possibly because referees subconsciously favor that person.

GOOD EATS

MCWEIRD

You pretty much know what's on the menu at McDonald's, unless you happen to travel to other countries. Then you may be quite surprised. Here is a sampling of some of the odd fare from McDonald's around the world:

Canada—McLobster lobster rolls are available in some regions.

Chile—instead of ketchup, they have avocado sauce for the burgers.

Costa Rica—beans and rice, a popular national dish, is offered.

Germany—beer is sold.

Greece—Greek Mac, a Big Mac in a pita, is popular.

Hong Kong—the burgers are not served between buns, but between glutinous rice patties.

India—the Maharaja Mac has either lamb or chicken. They also offer a veggie burger.

Israel—McKebob has Middle Eastern seasoning and is in a pita.

Japan—Ebi Filet-O shrimp burgers; Koroke burgers consisting of mashed potato, cabbage, and katsu sauce; Ebi-Chiki shrimp nuggets; and green tea milkshakes are available.

Norway—McLaks, which are grilled salmon burgers, are served with dill sauce.

 MCFLOPS

Some McDonald's American menu items that crashed and burned over the years included:

The Hula Burger, with pineapple slices instead of beef, which Ray Kroc thought would sell great during Lent, was introduced in 1963. The Filet-O-Fish proved a better bet.

The McPizza, which was available in the late eighties and early nineties, took too long to make for a fast-food joint.

The McLean Deluxe, offered in 1991, was 91 percent fat-free. They replaced the fat with water and used seaweed extract to bind the water to the beef, resulting in a very dry burger that consumers spurned.

Salad Shakers was a plastic box of salad which you added dressing to and shook up to mix. People didn't like having to scrape all the dressing off the lid of the container.

The McAfrika, which consisted of beef and veggies in pita, was introduced in Norway in 2002. At the time, there was a major famine occurring in Africa and human rights groups jumped all over McDonald's for its insensitivity.

Chicken Fajitas tanked because folks found them to be too small.

Ray Kroc prohibited any McDonald's from selling hot dogs, as he thought them unhygienic. After his death, some Midwestern franchises sold them as a summer item.

I WANT CANDY

People evolved to like sweets because most bitter things are poisonous.

Hershey's is the number one almond user in the United States.

M&M's are the number one candy in the United States, followed by Hershey's bars, Reese's Peanut Butter Cups, and Snickers.

Red M&M's were discontinued in 1976 because parents thought they contained a dangerous red dye, which they didn't. They came back on the market in 1987.

All M&M's colors taste the same.

Baby Ruth used to be called the Kandy Kake bar.

The New England Confectionary Company (NECCO) introduced NECCO wafers in 1912.

Wint-O-Green Life Savers spark when you bite them. So will two sugar cubes rubbed together.

The Dutch eat more candy than any other people.

Sugar Daddy was originally called the PaPa Sucker.

It takes 252 licks to get to the center of a Tootsie Pop.

Cracker Jack is the world's biggest user of toys, albeit small ones.

Charleston Chew is named for the Charleston dance that was popular in 1922.

Kit Kat came out as the Chocolate Crisp in 1935, but was renamed in 1937, after London's Kit Kat Club.

Chunky was named for creator Philip Silverstein's "chunky" baby granddaughter in 1936.

Junior Mints were named for a 1941 Broadway play—*Junior Miss*.

Three Musketeers debuted in 1932 and originally was three bars of different flavors—vanilla, chocolate, and strawberry—hence the name.

Snickers was introduced in 1930 and was named for a horse owned by the Mars family, the candy's makers.

Lollipop was originally the name of a racehorse.

David Clark first sold the Clark Bar on the streets of Pittsburgh in 1886.

Mounds is named for its shape.

MELTS IN YOUR MOUTH

White chocolate is not real chocolate. It contains only cocoa butter, sugar, and milk.

Chocolate melts at 77°F. The whitish "bloom" sometimes seen on chocolate is the cocoa butter rising to the surface.

There is naturally occurring lead in chocolate, and eating too much can cause mild lead poisoning.

DOUBLE BUBBLE

The average American chews about three hundred sticks of gum a year (some people don't chew any, but others chew a lot).

In 1919, to promote sales, Wrigley mailed four free sticks of gum to all 7 million of the households listed in American phone books.

Bubble gum is traditionally pink because it was the only color inventor Walter Diemer had on hand when he whipped it up in 1926.

THE JOY OF BAKING

Doughnuts have holes so the center cooks evenly.

Twinkies had banana filling until a shortage during World War II.

In devil's food cake, baking soda reacts with buttermilk to give the red tint.

Cupcakes got their name because the original recipe called for one cup of each ingredient.

Brown sugar is a mixture of granulated sugar and molasses.

To make pie, the Pilgrims cut the top off a pumpkin, filled it with apples, sugar, spices, and milk, put the top back on, and baked.

BUBBLY

Bud Light is the bestselling beer in the United States.

In 1962, Pittsburgh's Iron City Beer became the first canned beer with a pop-top.

The carbon dioxide in champagne helps to speed the alcohol into the stomach lining and blood.

Passing an electric field of six hundred volts through undrinkable raw, young red wine for three minutes shortens its maturation time and dramatically im-

proves its taste and drinkability. Wineries are anx-
ious to take avantage of this new technology as soon
as it's commercially available.

I SCREAM, YOU SCREAM . . .

Breyers is America's bestselling ice cream.

Brain freeze is triggered by the dilation of the vessels
in the head, triggered by a nerve on the roof of the
mouth.

It's the sugars, fats, and air bubbles in ice cream that keep
it from freezing solid.

People over fifty-five years of age eat the most ice
cream, as do New Englanders.

Frusen Glädjé means "frozen delight" in Swedish.
Häagen-Dazs means absolutely nothing.

CHEW ON THIS

In 2006, the Food and Drug Administration (FDA) ap-
proved the spraying of hot dogs and ready-to-eat meats
with viruses to kill *Listeria* bacteria.

More than 2,600 gallons of water are needed to create
a steak.

Muscles that do a lot of work store a lot of oxygen. This
is why chickens have dark meat on their legs and wings.
(Humans have dark meat too.)

Meat tenderizers work by breaking down the proteins in the meat, making it easier to chew.

Because a kangaroo emits six hundred times less greenhouse gas (methane) than a cow, some folks Down Under are pushing to replace beef patties with roo burgers.

UNDER THE SEA

The top three seafoods consumed in the United States are shrimp, canned tuna, and salmon.

It takes lobsters around seven years to reach the legal U.S. harvesting size of one pound.

That green gunk in lobster is the "tomalley," or the liver and pancreas, which filters crud out of the water. It can contain high levels of toxins.

Lobster blood is clear until cooked; then it turns into that white gunky stuff often seen floating in the pot of water.

Lobsters used to be so plentiful that they were a food of the poor in Colonial America.

Every so often, a bright blue lobster is found.

An Atlantic bluefin tuna can be worth as much as fifty thousand dollars, to a record one hundred thousand dollars.

Seven million Americans have seafood allergies.

GOOD EATS **229**

CHOWDAH

New Englanders shun tomatoes in their clam chowder. In 1939, a bill was introduced in Maine to make tomatoes in clam chowder illegal.

Manhattan clam chowder got its name from New Englanders, who considered it an insult to refer to someone as a New Yorker.

Restaurants usually don't serve both New England and Manhattan clam chowder.

EXPRESS AISLE

Piggly Wiggly opened the first self-service grocery store in 1916.

When the first shopping carts were introduced in 1937, people were reluctant to use them.

The first square-bottomed paper bag was used in 1870. Plastic shopping bags appeared in 1977.

People with big shopping carts buy 30 percent more food in the grocery store.

Consumers who shop with kids buy 40 percent more items.

BETTY, BEN, AND DUNCAN

Aunt Jemima is a fictional character based on an 1889 vaudeville dance tune.

Quakers have nothing to do with Quaker Oats. In 1877, a partner in the Ohio-based Quaker Mill Company thought that a Quaker on their logo would convey a wholesome image.

Uncle Ben was a black Texas rice farmer, renowned for his excellent crop. Converted Rice Incorporated appropriated his name and used Frank Brown, a restaurant maître d', for its logo and advertising.

Betty Crocker is a fictional character.

Duncan Hines was a restaurant guidebook writer in the 1930s.

Chef Boyardee was founded by Italian restaurateur—Hector Boiardi—in 1915.

DELICIOUS BEGINNINGS

Aunt Jemima was first sold as "Self-Rising Pancake Flour."

Philadelphia Cream Cheese used to be called Star Brand Cream Cheese.

When Frosted Flakes debuted in 1954, Tony the Tiger had a friend named Katy the Kangaroo on the cereal boxes.

In 1951, Jack in the Box became the first fast-food drive-thru.

Denny's began as Danny's Donuts in 1953.

Both Dunkin' Donuts and Howard Johnson restaurants started in Quincy, Massachusetts.

Kraft Macaroni and Cheese was the first prepackaged meal, in 1937.

THE GREATEST THING SINCE . . .

Otto Frederick Rohwedder invented the first bread-slicing machine in 1912, but bakers spurned it because sliced bread would go stale too quickly. In 1928, he invented a machine that would slice and wrap bread at the same time. A bakery in Chillicothe, Missouri, was the first to use it.

The color of the twist tie on bread may indicate which day it was baked on. Most bakers deliver bread to the stores on Monday, Tuesday, Thursday, Friday, and Saturday, and use twist tie colors blue, green, red, white, and yellow respectively to indicate which day.

CHEESY BITS

Pre-sliced cheese was first sold in 1947.

Monterey Jack cheese originated in Monterey, California, and was marketed by a guy named David Jacks.

It takes ten pounds of milk to make one pound of cheese.

PUT YOUR MONEY WHERE YOUR MOUTH IS

Well into the nineteenth century, Siberians could pay their taxes with garlic.

The Romans used to pay their legions in salt, or *salarium*, hence the word "salary."

During the Middle Ages, peppercorns were accepted as money.

VEGETABLE MATTERS

In the early nineteenth century, celery was a "classy" food. It was placed in the middle of the table as a centerpiece in a fancy pressed-glass celery vase.

Folks who harvest okra must wear long sleeves and gloves, as the leaves will cause a nasty rash that can last for weeks.

According to Pickle Packers International, there should be seven warts per square inch on American pickles, while Europeans don't like any.

V8 Juice contains beets, carrots, celery, lettuce, parsley, spinach, tomato, and watercress.

Asparagus spears can grow up to ten inches in one day.

Men eat more asparagus than women.

Nuns banned asparagus from girl's schools in the nineteenth century because of its phallic resemblance.

Carrots are native to Afghanistan and were originally purple or black.

Baby corn really is immature corn. It comes from special corn plants and is picked before the ears ripen to full size.

Only North Americans call corn "corn." Most of the rest of the world calls it "maize."

The most consumed foods worldwide, in order, are wheat, rice, corn, and potatoes.

Lima beans contain a cyanide compound that escapes as a gas when cooked. Certain types of lima beans are illegal in the United States for this reason.

Spinach was the first vegetable to be sold frozen.

When the Popeye cartoons were popular, spinach became one of kids' favorite foods.

Marilyn Monroe was crowned Miss California Artichoke Queen in 1947.

The first salad bar was at R. J. Grunts in Chicago in 1971.

Black-eyed peas, okra, peanuts, and watermelon all came to the New World with African slaves.

MOO JUICE

Echo Farms in Brooklyn was the first to put milk in bottles, in 1879. Before this, folks would buy milk from barrels on wagons and put it into buckets to take home.

Lactose is only found in milk.

Generally speaking, most people of northern European descent are not lactose intolerant, most of the rest of the world is.

NAME THAT FOOD

The kaiser roll was named in honor of Hapsburg emperor Kaiser Franz Josef.

Fettuccine Alfredo was created by 1920s Roman restaurateur Alfredo di Lelio.

Porterhouse steak is believed to have acquired its name from Martin Morrison's Porterhouse, a tavern that sold porter ale and specialized in this cut of beef.

A continental, or cold, breakfast gets its name from the fact that in England, a proper breakfast is hot and has meats and eggs, among other dishes. On the European continent, they favor a light meal of pastries and coffee.

Hush puppies are so named because hunting dogs in the South were fed fried cornbread balls to keep them quiet.

"Burrito" means "little donkey."

Oysters Rockefeller was named for John D. Rockefeller, by the owner of Antoine's in New Orleans.

Salisbury steak was created by Dr. J. H. Salisbury in the late 1800s. He recommended eating one three times a day for good health.

Fig Newtons were invented near Newton, Massachusetts, and are named for that town.

Baked Alaska was known as Alaska, Florida in the late 1800s.

Beef Stroganoff is of Russian origin and is likely named for a member of the powerful Stroganov family, probably the diplomat Count Paul Stroganov.

Boston baked beans were made a day ahead by the Puritans in the Boston area, who were forbidden to cook on the Sabbath.

Buffalo wings were first created at the Anchor Bar in Buffalo, New York, after they had received an overshipment of chicken wings.

"Squash" comes from *askutasquash*, the Narragansett Indian word meaning "eaten uncooked or raw."

EGGCELLENT TRIVIA

There is no difference between brown eggs and white eggs, save the color.

Chickens with red feathers and red earlobes (yes, chickens have ear lobes) lay brown eggs, those with white feathers and earlobes lay white eggs.

Brown eggs, laid by Rhode Island Reds, are most popular in the Northeast.

The average hen lays three hundred eggs a year.

SODA OR POP?

The word "pop" became associated with soda because early bottle caps made a "popping" sound when opened.

Folks in the Northeast, the Miami area, St. Louis, and parts of California call a carbonated soft drink "soda." Those in the Midwest, the Great Plains, and the Northwest predominantly say, "pop." In parts of the South, people are likely to use the generic term "coke," regardless of the soft drink they really want.

Pepsi used to be called "Brad's Drink," after its creator— Caleb Bradshaw.

7UP contained lithium until the 1940s and was originally called Bib-Label Lithiated Lemon-Lime Soda. (Lithium is used to treat bipolar disorder.)

RC Cola was the first soda sold in a can, in 1954.

Diet-Rite, in 1958, became the first diet soda.

The plastic (PET) soda bottle debuted in 1977.

Soda sold in PET bottles has "Drink By" dates because CO_2 can slowly seep through plastic, unlike glass bottles. (Half of all modern carpets are made from recycled PET bottles.)

Coca-Cola is the biggest end user of high-fructose corn syrup in the United States.

SUPER FOOD

In 1905, Lombardi's Pizzeria Napoletana, on Spring Street in New York City, became the first American pizzeria.

The top week for pizza sales is Super Bowl week.

GRILLIN'

Grilling is quick, hot cooking on an open flame. Barbecuing is slow, moist cooking involving adding sauce and smoking.

The charcoal briquette was invented by Thomas Edison and Henry Ford, as a way to make use of all the scrap wood left over from the making of cars.

Charcoal is made by grinding up wood and heating it to 1,800°F, creating a carbon substance known as char.

When it is mixed with coal and dried in molds, you get charcoal briquettes.

FANNY FARMER

The first cookbook to use actual measurements in recipes was *Fanny Farmer's The Boston Cooking-School Cook Book* in 1896. Before this, recipes specified a "pinch of this" and a "handful of that." Little, Brown only agreed to publish Fanny's cookbook if she put up the money for the printing of the first three thousand copies. The book went on to sell 4 million copies.

FUG ME? NO, FUGU.

The blowfish, or puffer fish, is the most poisonous vertebrate, after the golden poison frog.

> Puffer toxin is one hundred times more poisonous than cyanide. Ingestion can kill a person in one and a half hours. Poisoning victims become paralyzed but remain fully conscious as they slowly die of asphyxiation. There is no known antidote.

In Japan, puffer fish (*fugu*) is a potentially deadly delicacy. Only licensed *fugu* chefs are allowed to prepare it, after completing two to three years of extensive training.

WHEN IN . . .

In certain Bedouin tribes it is considered impolite *not* to burp vigorously after a good meal.

The Iranian confectioners union changed the name of the Danish pastry to "Roses of the Prophet Mohamed," after Danish newspapers printed cartoons depicting Mohamed.

MUTANT CHIPS

Green potato chips come from potatoes that while growing were exposed to sunlight and formed chlorophyll.

Dark brown potato chips come from potatoes that have been in storage too long and have high sugar content, leading to browning during cooking.

"ME WANT COOKIE!"

P. T. Barnum promoted Animal Crackers when they first came out in 1902, hence the circus motif packaging.

Oreos used to be made with lemon crème.

In 2007, due to concern over childhood obesity, *Sesame Street*'s Cookie Monster began calling cookies a "sometime food."

CREAMY OR CHUNKY?

The ancient Incas invented peanut butter.

America is the top peanut butter–eating country.

People on the East Coast prefer creamy peanut butter, those on the West Coast chunky-style.

Women and children prefer creamy; men, chunky.

The peanut butter and jelly sandwich was invented during World War II, when GIs combined the two from what they had in their rations.

> The average American kid will eat about fifteen hundred peanut butter and jelly sandwiches by the time of high school graduation.

Adults eat more peanut butter than do kids.

> Georgia is the top peanut growing state.

One-half of the U.S. peanut crop goes into peanut butter.

> Three million Americans are allergic to peanuts or tree nuts.

SOUP TO NUTS

Pistachios are colored red to hide blemishes.

> Campbell's soup cans were colored red and white after the Cornell football team in 1898. In 1900, the gold medallion was added to represent the medal the soup was awarded at the Paris Exhibition in that year.

NUTTIN', HONEY

Bees eat and regurgitate nectar numerous times to partially digest it.

There were no honeybees in America, until they were introduced from Europe in 1640.

Honey won't spoil, due to its high sugar content, which bacteria and fungi can't tolerate.

Honey was used to heal wounds in World War I. It absorbs moisture and dries out microbes.

I YAM A SWEET POTATO

Roughly 95 percent of the world's yams are grown in Africa.

The African slaves in America called sweet potatoes "yams" because they resembled African yams. The name stuck.

Unless you are shopping in an international market, it's likely you are buying sweet potatoes, as real yams are hard to find.

The U.S. Department of Agriculture requires labels with the word "yam" on them to follow it with the words "sweet potato," to avoid confusion.

LEFTOVERS

There are forty-nine different foods mentioned in the Bible.

Rapeseed oil is usually referred to as canola oil, for obvious marketing reasons.

About 90 percent of licorice is used by the tobacco industry to make cigarette smoke taste better.

Strawberry yogurt, grapefruit juice, and Good & Plenty are just a few of the foods that use ground-up female cochineal beetles and their eggs as a red food coloring.

Roughly 32 percent of the turkeys in the United States are eaten on Thanksgiving Day. Some 13 percent go into pet food.

The six thousand or so unemployed apple sellers on the streets of New York City, who became a symbol of the Great Depression, were rounded up and removed in 1931.

Crackers have little holes in them to let steam escape during baking, making them crisper.

Vegemite is a brown yeast extract paste that is a favorite breakfast food in Australia.

During a lifetime, a person will inadvertently eat several pounds of dirt.

Saint Martha (no, not that Martha) is the patron of cooks. She's the one who "served Jesus."

Welch's Grape Juice was created in 1869 as a nonalcoholic sacramental wine.

Gelatins are made from animal hooves, bones, and hides.

The British eat a steamed sponge pudding made of suet with currants called "spotted dick."

In 1980, Tyson Foods bred a special chicken just for McNuggets. It's called "Mr. McDonald."

Cheerios is the top-selling cereal.

WORST-CASE SCENARIOS

WORKING YOURSELF TO DEATH

In 2006, 5,703 Americans died on the job.

In 2007, commercial fishing was the most dangerous job, with 142 deaths per 100,000 workers. Slips and overboard falls are common on fishing boats off the coasts of Alaska, Massachusetts, and other seaboard areas. Right behind were pilots and aircraft engineers, with a death rate of 88 per 100,000 employees.

Logging is also extremely dangerous. Most fatalities are a result of falling trees.

Trash collectors and cabbies are more likely to be killed on the job than cops or firemen.

Twenty-five thousand people died building the Panama Canal.

DEATH BY ANIMAL

There are *only* one hundred shark attacks a year on average.

Deer are the most dangerous animals in America. In 2007, 223 people were killed when their cars struck deer. By comparison, only one person in the country was killed by a shark.

While hiking in the Rockies, you are more likely to be killed by a falling tree than by a grizzly bear attack.

SNOW DAZE

Snow and ice are directly or indirectly responsible for the injuries of thousands of Americans each year. In 2007, Americans suffered injuries while engaged in cold weather activities in the following numbers:

Snowboarding—57,972

Skiing—44,079

Shoveling snow—42,345

Ice skating—23,375

Ice hockey—18,679

Snowmobiling—12,735

Snow blowing—5,988

Snow tubing—3,464

MILITARY MAYHEM

In 2008, more U.S. Marines—twenty-five—were killed in motorcycle accidents than by enemy fire in Iraq.

Three-quarters of the world's population was drawn into World War II. More than 50 million people died as a result, including 38 million civilians.

A trained sniper, using a .50-caliber rifle, can kill someone from a mile and a half away.

There are eighty thousand amputees in Angola. Most got that way from the 8 million land mines that remain in the country following its civil war.

Worldwide, there are an estimated 100 million unexploded land mines.

MORE MAYHEM

The worst flood in recorded history killed an estimated 3.7 million people in 1931, when China's Huang He (Yellow) River ran amok. It has flooded at least fifteen hundred times since 2297 BCE, giving it the nickname "China's Sorrow."

An avalanche in the Italian Alps killed an estimated eighteen thousand in 218 BCE.

In December of 1916, during World War I, ten thousand Italian and Austrian troops died in avalanches in the Tyrolean Alps. During the course of the war, around sixty thousand were buried by the snow.

In 1970, an earthquake triggered a landslide in Yungay, Peru, that buried 25,000 people.

The deadliest earthquake in recorded history claimed 830,000 lives in Shansi, China, in 1556.

The biggest *accidental* oil spill ever was from a blowout on the Ixtoc I oil rig in the Gulf of Mexico in 1979, which released approximately 3.3 million barrels. By comparison, the *Exxon Valdez* spilled 257,000 barrels. The largest oil spill ever was caused when Saddam Hussein ordered the sabotage of the Kuwaiti oil fields in 1991. There is no hard data on the size of the release, but it was at least twice as big as the Ixtoc I, and probably much larger than that.

One hundred and five people were killed when an elevator at a gold mine in South Africa plunged more than sixteen hundred feet in 1995.

Forty-two people died when the cable supporting their ski lift at an Italian resort snapped in 1976.

Tornadoes, earthquakes, and floods kill about two hundred Americans a year.

Heat kills more Americans each year than all other natural disasters combined—more than four hundred.

During one week in July 1995, 739 Chicagoans died from heatstroke. Most were elderly people home alone. The Great Chicago Fire killed less than half that number.

At the same time of the Great Chicago Fire in 1871, there was a much more deadly forest fire taking place in the Michigan peninsula and north-eastern Wisconsin that killed more than eleven hundred people.

London Bridge burned down in 1212, killing three thousand.

Twenty-one people were killed and 150 injured in Boston when a 2.3-million-gallon tank of molasses ruptured and flowed through the streets in 1919. The area remained sticky and smelly for years afterward.

DEATH MOUNTAIN

The Annapurna is a group of six mountain peaks, all more than 23,600 feet, in the Himalayas of central Nepal, that are the deadliest for climbers, with a 40 percent mortality rate.

One in four of the climbers who reach the summit of K2, on the Pakistan-China border, die.

One hundred seventy-nine people have died climbing Mount Everest.

Forty-three people perished in an avalanche while mountain climbing on the Tajikistan-Kyrgyzstan border in 1990.

SIX FEET UNDER

Within three days after death, the enzymes in the stomach, which are used to digest dinner, start to digest the human body.

Each year, more than 827,000 gallons of formaldehyde, ethanol, and methanol from embalming fluids are buried in the ground in the United States.

Princess Diana is buried on a plot of land that used to be the family's pet cemetery.

In India, the Zoroastrians leave their dead out for a year to be consumed by vultures.

The oldest known mummies are those found high in the Andes on the Chile-Peru border and date to 6000 BCE. They are three thousand years older than those found in Egypt.

The Incas used to sacrifice and mummify children about five hundred years ago.

Eighty-four people are in cryopreservation (frozen) at the Alcor Life Extension Foundation in Scottsdale, Arizona.

DEAD-ON STATS

Men commit suicide more than women, but women attempt it more.

Approximately 80 percent of Americans die in the hospital.

Kentucky and West Virginia have the highest death rates from smoking. Hawaii and Utah have the lowest.

In human history, probably about 100 billion people have died.

DAY OF THE SKULLS

November 8 is Day of the Skulls in Bolivia, when folks honor the skulls of their dead relatives. Family members dress up the skulls and carry them to churches or cemeteries, where they are adorned with flowers and blessed.

Some people in Madagascar exhume their dead relatives and march their bones through their village in a ceremony called *famadihana*. The bones are then reburied with a new shroud and the old one given to a childless newlywed couple for their connubial bed.

WAY TO GO

Francis Gary Powers, the world famous U2-spy-plane and test pilot, died in 1977, when the television news helicopter he was piloting ran out of fuel and crashed.

Thomas Edison once electrocuted a full-grown elephant, on camera, to show that AC current was dangerous.

The first "witch" hanged in Salem, Massachusetts, met her fate on June 10, 1692. All told, nineteen were hanged, five died in jail, and one man was slowly pressed to death.

CRIME AND PUNISHMENT

WHACK JOBS

In 2006, 14,990 Americans were murdered.

The vast majority of murders are a result of arguments.

Approximately 42 percent of murder victims are killed by a family member or friend.

Good news for women—males accounted for almost 79 percent of murder victims in the United States in 2006. Men also did 66 percent of the murdering. Bad news for women—there were 92,455 cases of forcible rape in the same year. This does not include statutory rape or other offenses of a sexual nature.

New Orleans and Gary, Indiana, are the cities with the most murders per capita in the United States.

Louisiana has the highest state per capita murder rate, thirteen times higher than the rate in New Hampshire, which has the lowest.

AN EYE FOR AN EYE

Thirty-five states have the death penalty.

At the end of 2005, there were 3,254 American inmates sitting on death row.

Washington and New Hampshire still can hang people on death row.

Oklahoma's state medical examiner, Jay Chapman, proposed execution by lethal intravenous drip, which was first employed in 1977.

Folks in Erwin, Tennessee, once hung a 7,500-pound elephant after it was found guilty of murder.

Iran leads the world in child executions.

Eight countries have the death penalty for homosexuality.

Saudi Arabia, Qatar, and Yemen still permit beheading.

Some executioners during the French Reign of Terror said that they spoke to the bodiless heads within seconds of beheading and were able to elicit a response.

GETTING STONED

Stoning is perhaps the oldest form of capital punishment. Among the countries still allowing it are Afghanistan, Iran, Iraq, Saudi Arabia, Nigeria, the United Arab Emirates, Somalia, and Sudan.

In Iran and Yemen, nonlethal crucifixion is permitted as a method of punishment.

The Sudan, under their version of Sharia law, executed eighty-eight people by crucifixion as recently as 2002.

LOCKUP

Roughly 2.3 million Americans are locked up, more than in any other nation. By comparison, the country of San Marino has a total of one prisoner.

The state with the highest incarceration rate, by far, is Louisiana.

Fox Dix Federal Correctional Institution in New Jersey has the highest population of any U.S. prison.

CSI

The first gun linked to a crime by a bullet found at the scene was in London in 1835.

In 1891, the police in Buenos Aires were the first to use fingerprints to solve crimes.

The first crime scene tests on dried blood were conducted in 1915 in Italy.

In 1983, DNA evidence was first used, in an English court.

OLD-TIME JUSTICE

The Romans would crush a man's testicles if he were convicted of rape. A two-time offender would be castrated. The Greeks were no kinder, literally *pulling* the balls off the perpetrator. In more modern times, the French continued this form of punishment up until the Napoleonic era.

The Persians flayed Roman Emperor Valerian and had his skin turned into a footstool in 260 CE.

A seventeenth-century English judge could lock the jury in a room with no food or water until the desired verdict was reached.

CROOKED PYRAMID

Charles Ponzi, an Italian immigrant to the United States, created the Ponzi scheme in 1920. At one point, he was earning $250,000 a day. He died in poverty.

ONE SCAM TOO MANY

American financier Robert Vesco defrauded a mutual fund investment company out of $220 million in 1973, and flew a corporate jet to Costa Rica. He paid $2 million to Costa Rica's president to pass a law guaranteeing that he would not be prosecuted. In 1978, a new president repealed the law and Vesco fled to Antigua, where he tried to buy the island of Barbuda and start his own country. He lived with the Sandinistas in Nicaragua until moving to Cuba in 1982 for medical treatment. He got along with Fidel and Raul Castro, until he tried to scam Raul and landed in jail in 1995, where he remained until his death in 2007.

MOST WANTED

The FBI's Ten Most Wanted List was begun in 1950. Since then, 491 fugitives have been listed (eight of them women) and 460 have been captured. Of them, 151 have been caught with the public's assistance.

> The person who remained the longest on the list was alleged police murderer Donald Eugene Webb, who held the distinction for almost twenty-six years. He was removed from the list in 2007, without ever having been found.

Billie Austen Bryant only spent two hours on the list, in 1969.

> FBI agents didn't get to carry guns until 1934, twenty-six years after the bureau was formed.

BUM RAP?

Lizzie Borden was acquitted of killing her father and stepmother.

The house where the Borden murders occurred, in Fall River, Massachusetts, is now a bed-and-breakfast.

HOW WOULD YOU
LIKE YOUR CHANGE?

In 2004, a woman in Georgia was arrested for trying to pay for a purchase at a Wal-Mart with a million-dollar bill.

ACKNOWLEDGMENTS

I would like to thank my editor, Jeanette Shaw, for inviting me to take over the writing of this wonderfully useless trivia book series and for all her excellent insights and guidance. Also, thanks to Richard Willett and Jennifer Eck for their exceptionally thorough fact-checking. Thanks to Bryan Landsberg for a really cool cover. And as always, thanks to Janet Rosen for being such a great literary agent.

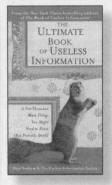